No More Frogs, No More Princes

WOMEN MAKING CREATIVE CHOICES AT MIDLIFE

Interviews by
Joanne F. Vickers, Ph.D.
&
Barbara L. Thomas, M.S.Ed.

The Crossing Press, Freedom, CA 95019

Acknowledgments

We would particularly like to thank the many women who have generously shared their stories and their lives with us. They have been a source of inspiration both for our work and our lives. Hearing these stories has been a great privilege.

We would also like to thank Sandra Joblonicky, who got us started and nagged us until we finished; Marty Ciccinelli, Pat Doust, Carol Haueter, and Richard North, who always kept us supplied with useful suggestions; Kathy Osterholm Graham, who gave us our first public forum for this work; Clare Lewandowski, Ann Malta, and Marilynn Strayer, who shared their professional insights about midlife women with us; Sue Bassani, Kay Bonham, Jennifer Diederich, Bill Heck, Liz Noe, Sandy and Jim Polen, Mary Jane Ryan, and Gaylon Vickers, who critiqued various drafts; Shelly Takei, Madeline Stein, Susan Whitten, who arranged interviews for us; Wally Leo, Peg Shackelford, and Karen Wilson and Joshua Mostow, who opened their homes to us; Nick Bova, Danny Stull, Jodi Thomas, and Gus Thomas, who provided us with computer support; Mary DeVore and Monica Ohlinger, who gave us suggestions about publishing; the women's groups who helped us early in the project to name the concerns and challenges of midlife women; and to our friends and families, who continued to ask, "How's the book?"

Finally, we would like to thank Elaine Goldman Gill and the staff of The Crossing Press, whose understanding and enthusiasm about our project has made this book a reality.

Library of Congress Cataloging-in-Publication Data

No more frogs, no more princes : women making creative choices in
    midlife / [edited by] Joanne F. Vickers and Barbara L. Thomas.
        p.   cm.
    ISBN 0-89594-626-2 (cloth). -- ISBN 0-89594-625-4 (paper)
crisis--United States--Case studies. I. Vickers, Joanne F.
II. Thomas, Barbara L. (Barbara Lee), 1939- .
HQ1059.5.U5N6 1993
305.24'4'0922--dc20

                                                    93-5283
                                                      CIP

———————

To our mothers,
Frances Rotundo Luckino (1910-1989)
      and
Arline Bradley Burger (1900-1988);
      and
Joanne's godmother,
Catherine Luckino Amato.

———————

Table of Contents

Preface

In fairy tales, the young woman must kiss a frog or wait for a prince in order for her life to be transformed. She is entirely dependent on situations and events outside herself for happiness.

No more frogs, no more princes means giving up the illusion that external situations and events will determine the direction of our lives.

The true prince lies within.

Stories distill the poetry of the person. From the early cave paintings of primitive tribes to television soap operas, stories have provided the shape and record of human culture. Our own stories capture our life experiences, and, as we remember and share these stories with others, they validate our life experiences.

The stories of others reveal possibilities for new shades of experience. When we face a crisis in our lives, we often seek out someone—a trusted friend or relative or character in a book—whose story can offer us consolation, hope, even a possible answer. Recognition of our own dilemma in another's story heals and restores us.

Most stories, however, whether psychological, social, historical, or fictional, have been written by men and have focused on men. In 1988, Carolyn Heilbrun noted that, until very recently, almost all biographies of women have been about the same women "almost always Gertrude Stein, occasionally Margaret Mead." The stories of Stein and Mead, while exciting, represent a small range of possibilities for women.

Another feminist writer, Carol Christ, explains how the absence of story affects women's lives: "Without stories there is no articulation of experience. Without stories a woman is lost when she comes to make the important decisions of her life. She does not learn to value her struggles, to celebrate her strengths, to comprehend her pain. Without stories she cannot understand herself."

Complicating this scarcity of women's stories is the fact that major studies of human development have paid little attention to the mature, midlife adult. Erik Erikson's personality theory about middle adulthood, which he extends from age twenty-five to age sixty-five, is a notable exception. But women themselves are taking their midlives seriously. The popularity of recent books like Cathleen Rountree's *Coming into Our Fullness: On Women Turning Forty* and Gail Sheehy's *The Silent Passage: Menopause* is evidence of how women are viewing this period as another chance to grow and develop.

The goal of this book is to give voice to real women whose stories provide models for growth between the ages of forty and sixty. It is not an academic treatise, a psychological study, or a political tract. It is the individual and collective story of women who meet everyday life head-on.

The women in this book belong to many different ethnic, racial, and religious groups. They live in different parts of the United States. Some have had the benefits of education and financial security while others have struggled without. All the women, however, have responded to midlife by looking within themselves to discover new directions for their lives.

For both of us, this book project began four years ago as a search for answers to questions about the puzzles and pains of our own midlife changes. Both of us faced health problems, career crises, and the deaths of our mothers in the same two-year period. We felt as though we had been transported to a new country without benefit of a guide or road map, let alone a language. We searched for books on midlife, but found little that inspired us.

We also began talking with women we knew who were our age or a bit older to talk about our mutual concerns. These women told us their stories; they encouraged us to collect midlife women's stories to share with others who were similarly searching for answers.

As we collected and studied these stories (and reflected on our experiences), we came to discover that midlife can truly be a creative and vital period. It is a time when women can reflect on their past and use their experiences to create identities of strength and integrity that can involve new perceptions, new work, new affiliations, even artistic expression. In Chapter 1, we explain more about the process of creativity and how it emerges as a powerful force in midlife. In the subsequent chapters, the women who have gone through this process tell their stories in their own voices. Most of the women wished to remain anonymous, so we have changed their names and, in a few cases, their locations. The women whose real names we have used are so indicated.

We hope you'll be as inspired as we are by the women of this book. May you face the challenges and possibilities of your midlife with courage and creativity.

Joanne F. Vickers
Barbara L. Thomas

Creative Choices
at Midlife

The ages between forty and sixty are a time of serious reckoning in a woman's life. They mark a journey into an unknown territory called midlife. This journey cannot be avoided, but the only signposts that may be familiar are negative ones, such as menopause and assorted fears of losing everything from memory to a firm bust-line.

Women wonder what to expect on this journey. Who can be relied on for help? How many wrong turns or missteps will have to be corrected? Will traveling the second half of life bring a sense of happiness and fulfillment or feelings of loss and regret?

The approximately twenty-eight million American women who are now between the ages of forty and sixty grew up and came of age in an era of rapid changes that have affected every facet of life. Those currently in their fifties may remember a time when divorce and even television sets were not part of the family scene, when mothers defined themselves solely as homemakers, and when fathers weren't too sure about the value of college for "girls." Career counselors, psychotherapists, even self-help manuals were largely unknown. Instead, many women put their trust in some mythical Prince Charming who was supposed to make them feel happy and fulfilled.

Women who are now in their forties and fifties experienced the pain and growth catalyzed by the civil rights movements of the 1960s. Many of them felt the fallout from Betty Friedan's "feminine mystique"; they rushed into the workplace to become superwomen who, as a popular television commercial of the 1980s promised, "could bring home the bacon and cook it, too." As the first sizable sandwich generation, they are currently coping as caregivers to both children and aging parents. These women reflect a time in American culture when societal roles and expectations have been drastically and repeatedly revised. And now they have entered midlife.

To discover some useful directions through this midlife territory, we collected the stories of many women who are making this journey. In the past four years, we have interviewed over one hundred women between the ages of forty and sixty about the experiences that characterize their midlife transitions.

We asked our interviewees such questions as what changes did you experience between forty and fifty, between fifty and sixty? Did you have a midlife crisis? What precipitated it? How did you feel about going through midlife? What happened to you as a result of this process? What does it mean to you to be in the second half of life? How would you define yourself now? How do you feel about yourself now?

Most denied having a "midlife crisis," which is understandable given the negative connotations of this term. Almost all of the women we interviewed, however, did admit to having a midlife reckoning experience.

For some women, the reckoning process took several years; for others, the transition was short-lived. The difficulty of this experience also varied— some women found it dramatic or painful, and others found it gradual or easy. Some women realized, as they were going through this process, that they were making significant changes in their perceptions of themselves and their goals in life. Others remembered or admitted to only vague feelings of dissatisfaction or unrest that kept nagging just below the surface; only in hindsight were they fully aware of the changes they had initiated.

We studied the stacks of notes and tapes from these interviews to look for common features in women's midlife experiences that we could share with other women who were concerned about coping with their own midlife journeys. We also turned to recent books by and about women in search of additional clues about midlife.

When we were rereading Carolyn Heilbrun's *Writing a Woman's Life*, this quotation jumped off the page at us. Heilbrun quotes Maxine Kumin's poem, "Archeology of a Marriage," in which Kumin says: "When Sleeping Beauty wakes up/she is almost fifty years old." No kiss from a handsome prince to wake her up? No perpetual youth? The myth-shattering truth of these two lines suddenly brought all of our research into sharp focus. Waking up at midlife! Waking up to a new life, creating a new life—this explained what we had been hearing from our interviewees.

And this resonated with our experience as well. Certainly, each of us was feeling more alive as we considered the changes we were in the process of making. The more we took responsibility for shaping our lives, the more vitality we seemed to have. We, like the women we interviewed, seemed to be crafting lives we wanted rather than simply continuing to cope with the lives we had. Waking up seemed to us a fitting metaphor for midlife change. It signifies that women are searching *within* for answers. They are no longer depending solely on outside influences to determine their lives: no more frogs, no more princes.

So what does waking up at midlife mean exactly? For the women we interviewed, the basic pattern of the awakening follows these lines: It begins with, at some level of awareness, facing, wrestling with, and accepting unavoidable changes in their lives whether they are physical, professional, psychological, social, or spiritual. Beyond that, it involves a process of self-assessment and self-discovery that includes finding the courage deep within to take risks to build a new life.

And, in some meaningful way, this new life focuses on personal satisfaction and achievement, on individual identity and self-esteem as important building blocks. Many women even go back and rediscover the dreams and ambitions they had for themselves as children and young girls, which they had forgotten about in the intervening years.

In fact, we were surprised by the number of interviewees whose girlhoods strongly influenced their creative choices at midlife. For example, Louise Bigmeat Maney came to accept her identity as a potter; she had learned and rejected pottery-making as a small child. And Kay Preston called on her childhood sense of adventure and innovation to survive after her divorce.

The real crisis of midlife, then, seems to be a crisis of identity and meaning, and creativity resolves this crisis. Answers to the questions "Who am I now?" and "What do I do now?" are resolved through a creative process that awakens women to new possibilities for being.

We observed that our interviewees made choices that fell into three different categories of creativity. The first group chose a traditional outlet in the arts, such as painting and pottery, to express who they are. These women feel that artistic creation helps them get in touch with and express something that is key to their being and thus gives them great joy.

The second group, the majority of women, became involved in new work and/or new affiliations. The affiliations may be personal, like marriage, or community-based, like volunteer work with AIDS patients. The core significance of this new work or new affiliation is that it is a choice based on a considered, mature sense of one's self—one's abilities as well as one's needs. These women also seemed to choose their new work or affiliation because it offers them the same sense of personal power and fulfillment that other midlife women find in artistic expression.

The third group of women focused on developing an inner life. They gave up money, ambition, and material goods to create a life that is inner-directed or spiritual. They rearranged their lifestyle to allow time for quiet reflection; they have a need to just be. For this group, creativity is as much about letting go as it is about taking on new ventures.

However midlife women express their creativity—the arts, new work or affiliations, inner-directedness—the result is that they become comfortable with who they are.

But how does one go about making creative choices? It is not within the scope of this book to provide an in-depth discussion on creativity. However, we wanted to provide a framework for readers that would explain how this creative process develops in relation to midlife change. We borrowed a paradigm from *The Creative Spirit* by Daniel Goleman, Paul Kaufman, and Michael Ray who divide it into four stages: preparation, incubation, illumination, and translation.

Preparation

During the preparation phase, a person gathers appropriate information and experience—the raw materials that creative energy will work with later. In a general sense, one's whole life up to midlife is a preparation for midlife creativity. The way women were raised, their experiences in school, their marriages, their work—all have helped to shape the persons they are today. As women approach forty, any change in a life pattern (marriage, health) precipitates the preparation phase in earnest.

Recent studies in the psychology of women acknowledge that men and women come to maturity in different ways. Jean Baker Miller's "new psychology of women" maintains that "Women stay with, build on, and develop in a context of connection with others....women's sense of self becomes very much organized around being able to make and then maintain affiliations and relationships." Men's maturation process, on the other hand, involves separation, individuation, and achievement. Psychologist Carolyn Gilligan agrees: "When women construct the adult domain, the world of relationships emerges and becomes the focus of attention and concern." Women's developmental process is grounded in a vision of reality that is based on affiliation and nurturing relationships.

In accommodating themselves to others and focusing on relationships, however, women may neglect building a sense of themselves as distinct and valuable individuals. At midlife, a woman's most obvious sense of herself may be in terms of her relationships with others as daughter, wife, mother, employee. When she realizes this, the question of who she is *apart from* these relationships often becomes a nagging one.

For these women, the process of emancipation and individuation can be quite painful. This is particularly true when the relationships a woman has centered herself around change, become less fulfilling, or disappear altogether. Ann Malta, a family therapist in Columbus, Ohio, confirms that women often first start therapy in midlife because the relationships they have attuned themselves to for so many years do not offer an "opportunity for personal growth...and these women have lost a sense of themselves."

Another catalyst for the preparation phase may be an awareness of aging. This awareness may begin when women realize they can no longer lose those extra ten pounds by dieting for a couple of weeks. Or when they start to think seriously about how much money they need to save for retirement. Or even when they discover that going to bed early with a good book is probably going to be more satisfying than a night on the town.

For other women, their sense of mortality becomes dramatized by sudden personal illness or the totally unexpected illness or death of a friend or relative. As of this writing, medical research claims that one in eight American women will develop breast cancer. In *Revolution from Within*, Gloria Steinem writes about how her experience with cancer forced her to begin to deal with entering midlife.

The preparation phase thus begins when women approaching midlife become aware of the limitations of their relationship roles and their physical limitations. A sense of urgency may grow: It becomes important to women to do something meaningful and satisfying with the remainder of their lives.

Incubation

Information and experiences gathered in the preparation phase sink into the unconscious where they incubate and grow into new ideas and images. Nothing needs to be done to make the unconscious process information; it just does. However, some activities seem to give the unconscious a better opportunity to work than others.

Incubation is a time for daydreams, meditation, and prayer. It is a time for suspending judgments and rational thinking and just being. Incubation requires both relaxation and receptivity. It involves putting worries aside for a while, perhaps temporarily accepting the anxieties of not having a clear solution to a problem. It might also involve some playful or relaxing activity, such as going to a movie with a friend, gardening, or throwing a dinner party. Engaging in some activity that is totally unrelated to the problem allows the solution to "cook" at an unconscious level.

In explaining the relationship between the unconscious and creativity, psychologist Rollo May describes "the constructive use of solitude," which allows our insights to take shape. After years of responding to the needs of others, many women need time just to be with themselves. Analyst Jean Shinoda Bolen encourages women to experience "the deliciousness of solitude." She says, "We must have solitude. Often, it is out of those moments that our creative impulses come."

One of our interviewees recalls a place in the mountains near Phoenix, Arizona, where she would go alone to meditate. Another woman spent time just sitting in her backyard garden, and it was there that she began to become clear about what she needed to do with her life.

Although this stage does invite rest, it can also be a period of discomfort as women wait for clarity about what needs to be changed. Husbands and children, even friends, ask, "What's wrong with you?" The media bombards women with messages that tells them to be active and feel good. Waiting for an answer, being still with themselves is not culturally encouraged. But it is essential to well-being.

Illumination

The answer to many soul-searching questions comes like the proverbial bolt from the blue—the aha! experience. Actually, it surfaces from the unconscious where it has been incubating. The solution seems clear, and women may initially respond to it with certainty and excitement. Some of our interviewees had strong illumination experiences: "I woke up one morning, and I just knew"; "It just came to me all of a sudden"; "When I finally realized what I had to do, I just walked out that door and haven't stopped since."

Many interviewees talked about an awakening experience that both delighted and frightened them. They were delighted with the discovery, but frightened about the changes and risks it involved. The illumination itself may trigger yet another period of anxiety and uncertainty, another period of preparation and incubation. In fact, this pattern of preparation, incubation, and illumination may be repeated several times over a period of months or years.

Awakening to a new reality can involve conflict for midlife women. It requires changes in expectations both of themselves and of others in their lives. Women may even collude with family and friends to maintain the status quo. They have become comfortable in their old roles even if these roles no longer fit. Change is uncomfortable and uncertain.

Becoming who one really is requires leaving home if only in a metaphorical sense. Even if women recognize that a leavetaking is in their best interest, they may have a variety of reasons for remaining attached to past roles, for playing it safe. If leavetaking means pursuing new interests that involve letting go of nurturing roles, women may feel guilty and disoriented.

During this time, women may again seek solitude or engage in long talks with trusted friends about what they are feeling. They may seek out books on self-help and personal growth. They may attend classes and workshops on personal growth or enter into therapy for the first time. Childhood wounds may need healing before women can move on. Whatever resources they seek in this process, women must go inside themselves for the answers to who they are. However, as they savor the newly awakened sense of self, it becomes easier to consider taking risks.

Some women find ways to take safe risks—to test the waters with their ideas. For example, three of our interviewees made geographical moves to places of perceived safety before they took the next steps. Several others took a single college class before making any commitment to a degree program.

In *Revolution From Within*, Gloria Steinem acknowledges the difficulty of life change: "We hurt both ourselves and other people when we become who they want us to be instead of who we really are. Nonetheless, the prospect of getting unhooked from this obsession sometimes creates as much anxiety as giving up any addiction."

Sometimes, women may get stuck in one of these stages and feel unable to move on in their journey. Feelings of uncertainty and resignation may overwhelm them. Women can draw hope in this situation by recognizing that possibilities for change exist which simply haven't occurred to them *yet*. Simply reminding themselves of this fact can be enough to set the process in motion once again.

Finally, women seem to arrive at a very basic reality; they speak to themselves with a voice that says: "Yes, we are getting older, yes, we have a limited lifespan, but we have survived for forty or more years. We have survived the traumas of teenage dating, school, marriage, mothering, working, and everything else that life has thrown at us." Somehow, this knowledge gives women the conviction that they can continue to survive, that they can handle inevitable, perhaps unpleasant changes.

More importantly, women begin to realize that they have the courage to initiate change on their own and to take risks to achieve desired change. Psychologist Marsha Sinetar confirms, "Letting go of all that is dear or familiar can be our starting point of power. When we leap into an abyss in order to honor life...we experience rebirth as a larger, mysteriously expanded self."

Translation

In this final phase of the creative process, women put their illuminations into action. Like Kumin's Sleeping Beauty, they have awakened to new possibilities for self-esteem, identity, achievement, and satisfaction.

Having realized who they are and how they must be to express themselves honestly, they take risks to make these ideas a reality. The risks often demand courage, especially if major changes are required, such as leaving a bad marriage, applying for a business loan, committing to a new lifestyle.

Facing these risks, however difficult, is worthwhile because doing so provides an affirmation of the self, a renewed vitality combined with an appreciation for maturity. These risks come from a deep sense of the self that is not possible in youth. Moreover, this stage of translating ideas into action has a synergistic effect: We often noted in our interviewees lives that, once they took a risk to change their lives, other opportunities and directions opened up to them.

Our experiences support this synergistic effect. When we began research for this book, Barbara awakened to how much of her sense of herself had become submerged in her role as a caregiver in both her professional and personal life. Working with ideas resurrected her intellectual and creative side that had been inhibited in affiliative roles. Halfway through the book, Barbara leased an office, "a room of her own," where she could concentrate on her thinking and writing. She also began to offer workshops on mindful living, which developed out of an appreciation of the ordinary that solitude brought her.

Joanne rediscovered how much writing had meant to her many years ago before she started raising a family as a single parent and teaching college. As the joy of writing took hold again, she decided to pursue another lifelong interest, making jewelry. She started taking classes working with metals, gems, and beads and discovered how satisfying it is to work with her hands. Centering her life around what had meaning for her rather than simply reacting to what was expected of her became important to Joanne.

Essentially, in the translation process, women can use their experience of nurturing others to give *themselves* sustenance, to enable their own growth processes. Writer Robert Grudin notes that creativity is a "radical act of freedom"; it is the freedom to become ourselves. And as with any creative process, as we women give shape to our midlife identity, we realize a sure joy, a grace, and a sense of rightness with ourselves and the world. It is in midlife that women can come to understand and shape their own stories.

The Fall into Grace

Sandra Lebold

> Change is a necessary part of life. It's a challenge.
> If you never let go of memories or people or experiences,
> you can never move on....If you give up one thing, it
> seems two or three other things show up to replace it if
> you only look for them.

Childhood physical and sexual abuse usually marks an individual for life. Betrayal by parents leaves painful scars that, even years later, can prevent a person from developing feelings of self-worth or forming intimate relationships. Healing requires courage and can be a long, difficult process.

Crippling accidents can similarly mark individuals with despair. Recovery can be agonizingly slow, and healing the physical pain and emotional fears caused by the accident requires tenacity and determination.

Sandra Lebold has experienced both of these traumas. She is a survivor of physical and sexual abuse by her father and abandonment by her mother. And, at age thirty-seven, she had a near-fatal accident that required a long recovery. But Sandra has been able to work through these painful experiences on her own. At forty-six, she has become a successful oil painter, romance novelist, gallery owner, and art teacher.

As a painter, she is well known as a creator of lush, colorful garden and forest scenes that owe their existence more to fantasy than to any real world. She has been shown in several galleries and, at the time of her interview, was preparing canvases as part of a major three-person show. In cooperation with two other artists, she is preparing a grant proposal that seeks funding to develop a show focusing on the experiences of artists who have been abused in their childhoods.

She also has solid business partnerships with two close women friends. With one, she owns and manages a fine arts gallery; the other is her novel-writing partner.

Sandra's story is a testimony to the remarkable healing potential of creativity. Sandra has never had any psychotherapy to deal with her childhood abuse. She did not discover her creative ability until her accident; her lengthy recovery provided time to develop new talents.

Painting opened up a new vista for Sandra. Even though she had no art train-
ing, she found that she had a fertile imagination that she enjoyed using. In the years
since her accident, she has learned to trust herself enough to exploit her creativity in
other fields, such as writing and running a business. As long as Sandra can see her
work in creative terms, she feels fulfilled as well as challenged.

Sandra invites us to her gallery for our interview where we are surrounded by
a rich variety of color and media: paintings, fiber arts, ceramic designs, and jew-
elry. Sandra herself creates a striking impression. She is a slight woman with large
brown eyes and a soft cloud of dark hair that falls to her shoulders.

The black jacket she wears over a beige knit dress has a scattering of antique
rhinestone brooches. Some are pinned along one sleeve—a dramatic gesture that
gives the impression of a woman who creates her own style. When she speaks, a
trace of country twang remains in her voice. The accent hangs like a question mark
against the background of sophistication.

Sandra Lebold

I was born in a shack in South Carolina. My father made $67.50 a month, and we gave $6.70 of that each month to Oral Roberts. There wasn't much left. When I was nine years old, my mother left us—me and my sister Carol. We were the last of nine kids.

I had always wanted a beautiful porcelain doll—the kind with curly hair you could comb and eyes that opened and closed, but we were too poor to afford one. When my sister and I woke up that morning, two dolls were sitting on the couch. We couldn't believe they were real. We stood there for a long time just looking at them. Then we saw the notes from mom pinned on their dresses with a safety pin. I couldn't read real well, but I figured it out. My mother had left during the night, and, in her place, she had left these wonderful dolls.

Carol and I didn't say a word to each other. I took her hand, and we went into the kitchen where my daddy kept his tools, and we took out a hammer and a hatchet, and we went back into the living room. We looked at the dolls one more time, and then we...we killed them. After it was done, I started to cry because I realized that I didn't have either the doll or my mother. My sister and I never spoke about it again.

It wasn't too long after she left that my dad started beating and sexually abusing me. He hadn't ever done it before mom left. There was no one I could tell. Everybody in town called my daddy "Uncle Billy." Everybody just loved him.

Whenever I did something wrong, he would say, "You need a whipping, but I'm not going to give it to you now." Then in the middle of the night, he'd wake me up with a belt in his hand and start beating me. Other times, though, he would sexually abuse me. I know he also abused other twelve- and thirteen-year-olds from the neighborhood. If I came home from school too early, I'd see him in bed with a girl. He would give them candy or money or something. There wasn't a day that I didn't think of committing suicide.

When I was twelve, Carol and I learned that mom was working at a motel, and we skipped school to go see her. We hadn't seen her in all those years. We hid behind a tree and watched her clean a room, come outside and shake her dust mop, and then move on to another room. We were too afraid just to go up to her, so we figured out a plan to meet her. We just knew that, if she could see us, she would love us again.

The next day we skipped school again and walked seven miles to the head of the bus line. We sat in back where we could see everybody get on. When she got on the bus, Carol ran down the aisle right away yelling, "Mom, mom, it's me, Carol!" She looked at us—she was such an old-looking woman wearing a patched coat—and then, right away, she pulled the emergency string and got off the bus.

That's the day I realized that no matter how smart I was, or how nice I was, I wouldn't ever be able to depend on her. Nothing I did would ever make a difference to her. I really had a lot of anger for her because she *had* to know what kind of man she had left us with. Whenever my dad whipped me or molested me, I thought about her, and I blamed her. I thought about how much I hated her. Her betrayal was really harder for me to get over than what my dad did to me.

Finally, one of my older sisters came and got me when dad said he was going to marry me off to a thirty-five-year-old widower with six kids. I lived with her and finished high school. I was the first one in my family ever to finish high school.

I got married when I was nineteen. There was really no feeling of love between us even though we were best friends. I guess I was just looking for an escape from my family problems. Dad died suddenly shortly after we got married. I never confronted him about what happened. I never saw my mother again either.

I had two beautiful kids, lived on a two-hundred-acre farm, and felt grateful to have escaped. I even went back and got my sister Carol and helped her finish high school.

I never did have any therapy for the abuse. I wish it hadn't happened, but, somewhere along the line, I just realized that I wasn't to blame for what happened. I was a child, and the situation was completely out of my control.

I put the blame where it belonged and just let it go. I haven't carried it since.

I was married for eighteen years. I enjoyed being a farm wife. We had a beautiful eleven-room house. Then one day I fell forty feet from a barn loft onto an oak hardwood floor.

When I fell, I broke both my legs and my ankles, my pelvis was crushed, my lower spine was in trouble, I needed two kidney surgeries—one right away, one later. At first, the doctors weren't sure I'd make it.

Then they told me I'd probably never walk again—at least not without some kind of support, maybe I'd need a wheelchair. I spent months lying flat on my back in a hospital bed and looking up at the ceiling. I could move my head twelve degrees, and I had limited use of my arms and hands. That was it.

When you lie there day after day, night after night, you begin to believe what the surgeons tell you. I started to wish I had died. I became a real bitch to people who tried to help me. Nothing they did was right; it wasn't done the right way because I couldn't get up and do it.

I had a friend who was a painter, and she came one day, and she said, "Sandra, you're becoming a bitch." I said, "I know, but I don't know what to do about it. They come in here and turn out the lights and say, 'Go to sleep,' and I can't sleep because I've been laying here all day. My days and nights are all mixed up. I've got bedsores from laying here in bed. I'm in pain all the time, and the mental pain is even worse. I just feel imprisoned in all this plaster. I'm imprisoned in a body that won't do what I want it to do."

She said, "I'm going to teach you to paint." And I told her, "'I don't want to." She just said, "Shut up, I'm going to teach you to paint." She turned out to be a true friend.

She and my husband built an easel that slanted horizontally over my bed, and she gave me lessons. She wouldn't pay any attention to all my protests about how stupid all this was, trying to paint upside down.

I first started to paint just to get her off my back because she would nag me and nag me. After that, somewhere along the line, I found out that I loved it. I would paint from morning when I woke up until night. Every once in a while, someone would have to clean me up with turpentine because I had oil paint all over my face and my gown. The paint would just drip on me.

Slowly, I found out that, if you use your mind, you can go anywhere you want, you can be with anybody you want, you can do anything you want in fantasy, in reality, in color, anything you want. If your mind can do it, you can do it. So being in that hospital bed was no excuse for me becoming the bitch I was turning into.

In the beginning, learning to paint was really just a therapy. But I discovered a love for it. I had never been artistic, had never taken any kind of training or classes. But I made up pictures in my head to get me through this bad time. The painting got me through. After twenty-two months of physical therapy and more surgery, I was back on my feet.

I became an emergency medical technician volunteer on an emergency squad. I felt it was payback time. So many wonderful people took care of me when I had the accident—like nurses who would sit and hold my hand while I cried because of the pain. The emergency squad experience really confirmed for me how fragile life is and how wonderful people can be in a crisis. It helped me realize that not all people are mean and take advantage.

I wanted to continue with my painting when I got well, but my husband thought I should put the easel away and go back to being a farm wife and mother. I couldn't do that. We couldn't find a compromise, so we got divorced. A couple of years later, I married again, but I found out that my husband was a drug user. When he refused help, I realized this was something I didn't need to waste my time on. I left.

I've never felt selfish about going on with the painting. I had never had any opportunity to develop myself, never had any training in painting, so I figured this was my time. It was long overdue. I thought about how far I could have come if I had started painting at seventeen instead of thirty-seven. I needed to see what my potential was. I couldn't go back to being a housewife who only had her soap operas to look forward to.

My pride and joy is being an art teacher. Some of my students have been with me for more than four years now, and they are starting to win top awards at major shows. I enjoy passing on to other people my love of color and creating things.

I also enjoy working with all kinds of artists in our gallery—painters, weavers, jewelers, potters. I even enjoy designing the showcases and windows. It's creative work.

I like to set new goals for myself. Four years ago, I decided I wanted to learn to play a long-time favorite song on the piano even though I had never played the piano before. It's an old country song. It's called "I'm Not Jessie." You probably never heard of it. I bought an old second-hand piano and started with little tunes like "Twinkle, Twinkle, Little Star" and "Good King Wenceslas" until I moved up to "Jessie." I practiced that song every day until it sounded right and I felt good about it. Then I was done, so I sold my piano.

Two-and-a-half years ago, I decided I wanted to try my hand at writing romance novels. A good friend and I decided we'd do it together—share the writing and the research. We published one novel last year, and we have a contract for a second one. I'm working on a deadline right now.

I guess I'm not a person who can direct her energies in just one direction. I like to pursue lots of openings. I'm never bored. Everything I do I love. I'm just lucky my loves are the ways that I earn my living. Real success is wanting what you have, and that's where I am, and I know it.

Right now, I have a real comfortable relationship with another artist. He's very supportive of me, and I support him even though we sometimes nag at each other for all the time we put into our work. But he understands how important it is for me to do what I'm doing. And I appreciate how committed he is to his work. We are equals.

When I feel rotten, I sit down and talk to myself. I'm a great talker to myself. I tell me how lucky I am, and I count my blessings. I know that sounds hokey, but it works for me. What does it matter if one little piddly thing goes wrong when I know I have what I think is most important—and that's doing what I want to do.

When I think about the future, I think I should try to slow down a bit because I'm on the go sixteen hours a day. But then I think about all the things I want to do. I want to try sculpture. I'd love to learn how to weld, so I could try metalworking. I want to travel, so I can search out some good locations for the novels I want to write in the future.

Change is a necessary part of life. It's a challenge. If you never let go of memories or people or experiences, you can never move on. When something has served its purpose, it's time to move on. Life can always be exciting. If you give up one thing, it seems two or three other things show up to replace it if you only look for them. Change forces you to grow as a person. I always want to be open to moving on.

Although I don't believe in organized religion, I'm a very spiritual person. I believe there's a special piece some people call God in every person. Some people get in touch with it, and some people don't. I got in touch with it when I came so close to dying. When you are well one minute and all broken up and in the hospital the next, your perspective changes. I know I'm a strong person.

I've used my experiences to motivate me to accomplish what I want to do. It was hard to see it at the time, but that fall in the barn was the best thing that could have ever happened to me.

That Newspaper Lady

Kay Preston

> Yoga was a life-changing experience for me....it was the
> beginning of looking inside myself for answers instead
> of outside myself. I began to recapture something im-
> portant that had been there all along, but had been re-
> pressed. It gave me a lot of freedom.

As young girls, women were full of ideas and dreams. They initiated projects and explored new vistas. They were interested and involved in the world around them and were often strong presences to be reckoned with.

According to Emily Hancock in A Girl Within, girls are often cut off from complete identity development in pre-adolescence just as they are becoming most fully themselves. Around the age of eleven or twelve, many girls find their interests restricted by adults who urge them to focus their attention on activities that are traditionally defined as feminine.

Individual interests may get put on the back burner, perhaps for the next thirty or forty years. When women reach midlife, however, they can sometimes shed this socialized self and regain that primary part of themselves left behind in childhood.

Kay Preston did just that. Following a divorce in midlife, she rediscovered the ingenuity and confidence she had as a girl and began to rebuild her life.

As a child, Kay was a free spirit—a tomboy allowed to roam the small Texas town where she grew up. A scholarly aunt served as Kay's mentor and fueled her growing intellect.

When Kay married in the early 1950s, she threw herself into her roles of wife and mother. After taking a part-time job as a librarian, she worked at her domestic roles even harder to avoid being criticized for neglecting her family.

Her decision to take back her life ended the marriage, but she approached her new independence with a sense of adventure. Because of her willingness to make painful and difficult choices, Kay, now sixty years old, lives a life true to her own values and needs.

Kay is an open and hospitable woman, and her home mirrors her gracious-ness. The living room where we talk is comfortable. Bird prints and modern art pieces reflect her diverse interests. A large bookcase full of books dominates one wall in the room. As she talks, Kay's old collie dog lies faithfully at her feet.

Kay Preston

I grew up in a very interesting home, a home for which I have great respect as I look back. I was the youngest of three daughters. My parents were older than most, and I sort of went my own way. I grew up in a small town in Texas that gave me many advantages because I had a lot of freedom. I could do a lot of experimenting in a safe context.

I was similar in many ways to Scout in *To Kill a Mockingbird*. I would sort of pop in on Saturdays wherever I happened to be, and somebody fed me. Nobody really worried about me. I wandered around a lot. In Texas, there is enough space for you to be quite individualistic without stepping on some-body else's toes. I like that in retrospect because I grew up with a lot of individualistic people.

I was quite different from anybody else in my family, and I think I was an enigma to them. I have one surviving sister, and I still don't think she knows much about who I am.

When I look back at me at ten or eleven, it is like having a joyful re-union with that girl. I have a picture of me at that age that moves me to tears because I think "What a great kid! What's not to like?" She was fantastic, open—that sort of thing.

Perhaps the more confident you are, the bigger swing you make when you realize that, as a girl, you aren't going to get anywhere in society. I had a stormy, rebellious, dangerous adolescence. I thank God that I didn't live in the era of drugs. I was very angry without insight into why I was angry.

My father was very socially conscious. He was trained as a dentist in the army. He read a great deal, but too much education was suspect in our fam-ily. Mother was a very cultured woman who could have joined an opera troupe at one time, but her father thought that was no fit life. She knew a lot about music and books, and she spoke flawless English.

I had conflicts with my mother that my sisters didn't have. She would say things to me like, "You're the only child I had I couldn't like." I now realize my mother was filled with a lot of rage. She had tried to be a boy to please her father. She had great potential and had been cut off.

My oldest sister was very accomplished academically. My middle sister had a very painful life. She finally died at the age of forty-one of alcohol and drug addiction. So...I went my own way. Nobody really talked to me about anything.

I had an aunt who was a Latin scholar who had been widowed young. She lived with my grandmother across the street. My aunt was considered too intellectual by most people in the family. She was a real mentor to me. She guided my reading and had many conversations with me. She didn't get impatient with me about my theories and ideas. Her son found her very difficult, but she was very good for me.

Going away to Stephens College was the first real life-changing experience for me. There were girls from every state in the U.S. and many foreign countries in a student body of about sixteen hundred. Girls from the Southwest were very popular because we were so friendly.

I met a lot of people. I saw my first ballet and my first opera. I had dinner with Eleanor Roosevelt when she came to speak at the campus. College was an exhilarating experience. I couldn't get enough of it. It was wonderful to be in classrooms where the girls weren't acting silly because boys were there. And the teachers took us seriously. My life was never the same—I never wanted to go home again.

I was married at nineteen after a whirlwind courtship. He was on his way to the army during the Korean conflict. While he was overseas, I went home to Texas to finish my library degree at East Texas University. After that, I went back to Stephens College to work as a librarian.

I had two daughters by the time I was twenty-three and was able to stay home in their early years. I set about being the best mother that had ever been. I created a life that I thought was the right one to live. I had read a great deal, so I had an idea about how it was in other families. I tried to write a scenario and adopt it as my own and pretend it was real.

I always worked very hard and achieved a lot, but I went through periods of real depression—times when I couldn't clean house, couldn't decide what to wear. I have memories of pervasive fatigue.

I went to a psychiatrist who told me all my Rorschach interpretations were from books. That was my reality. I had several counselors after that, but I think my expectations were wrong. I was looking for a cure—an answer outside myself. But I did begin to become aware that I had really had a great time as a child, and I didn't anymore. As a woman, I faced a lot of pain, and confusion, and striving, and trying, and I never was satisfied. I became extremely goal-oriented without much attention to daily pleasures.

I went back to work part-time at a local library. I was being carried along and took advantage of whatever opportunities presented themselves. I had no real inner direction except for an unconscious, intuitive desire to get somewhere—to do something. Just kind of taking whatever came along, without any conscious commitment.

When I went back to work, I worked myself silly. We always sat down to a big dinner. I never let my children take bought cookies to Girl Scout meetings. I didn't want people to think the girls were neglected because I worked. Our lives centered around the children. We were regarded as a highly successful family. No one would have guessed the marriage would end in divorce.

I began to develop some serious health problems when I was thirty-eight or thirty-nine—colitis and general malaise. The doctor warned me that my condition was serious and that I should think long and hard about my present situation. He asked me to consider whether I could change or change my situation. "Or," he said, "you may die."

All the dreams I had around that time were of suffocating—and of elevators that went all the way up through the ceiling. I would come out in a totally unknown land with no sense of direction. I knew that I was very unhappy.

There comes a time when, if a marriage is not a good fit, it is legitimate to leave it. But it was a very painful thing to do. My mother was horrified. Everybody was. When I told my mother I was getting a divorce after twenty-two years of marriage she said, "Then you won't be any good to anybody." It was startling to me, but that is what I had always believed, too.

My husband was a very good man. Very strongly into women's rights—politically liberal. A good father. But it was also very important for him to control, and we were on a collision course. Money was power. That was very important to him. His way of showing affection was to buy me something. We discussed it, and he said he didn't want to make any changes and I thought, "I don't want to die," so I got out of it. I was forty-one—married twenty-two years when we divorced.

I went to New Jersey and joined the library faculty at Drew University. I bought a house that, on paper, I could afford. And I loved it. I had never balanced a checkbook. I had never seen a tax form. I often had not even endorsed my own paycheck. I had had no involvement in decision-making about money at all except that I spent a lot, more than I would have had I been given the facts.

I soon found that I could make the house payment, but I needed more money for other things. I needed about $200 a month more than I was making. That's when I took the paper route.

I saw an ad in the paper for a part-time job delivering papers in a very wealthy area of town. I called a man named Mr. Holm, an ex-marine. He was very gruff. He said, "Meet me at the train station at 4:30 tomorrow morning," so I met him. We talked for a few minutes. He looked at my jeep, then he hired me.

It was a wonderful confidence-building experience. For a year, I got up at 4:10 a.m. in very, very cold weather. Drove to the train station and listened to all-night talk shows and early morning music on the radio. If it was raining, I had to fold the papers and put them in plastic bags.

The deliveries were all to secluded estates and homes. I thought I would never learn the route. The first few times I went out, I was so scared I was nauseated. Gradually, I became good at it, and I came to enjoy it. I met the same people on the road every morning—like the milkman. A whole other world. Mr. Holm called me once and said, "People are calling me and saying they want the paper and they want that woman."

One morning, I startled one of the customers when I threw the paper near her as she was coming out of her garage. We began to talk, and she told me she was up early because she had to drive to Massachusetts for parents' weekend at Smith College. I said, "Maybe I'll see you there later because I'm leaving for there this morning, too."

I'll never forget the look on her face as it dawned on her what I was saying—that my daughter was also at Smith. I could see her processing that information. She was gracious and said, "Well, I hope I do see you!" She went on to tell me she was an insomniac and that, whenever I saw a light on in her kitchen, to come in for a cup of coffee. I never did. But I did see her in the course of that weekend, and I think that story spread in the community.

I had quite a schedule that year. After delivering the papers, I would go home, take a scalding shower, eat a huge breakfast, and be at my desk by 8 A.M. I would take my money every month and put it in one of my books because I had never dealt with cash before. I needed the route for about a year. I quit after I got a raise at the library.

In 1974, I married Peter, a man I had met many years before. I got to know him again after he moved to New Jersey to work on an experimental education project.

A year later, I went back to graduate school. I was scared to do this. Really scared. Because I thought, "I'm older. I'll never be able to get through it. I can't stay up late. I can't concentrate." But I did quite well.

After working all day, I'd get on the Erie Lakawana to ride into Hoboken. Get off at 14th Street and walk to the school. Then, I'd leave school after 10:30 at night and walk back down 14th Street to the train. People were sleeping in the station, rats were running around. I would get home about 11:30.

I did this alone, at least once a week, sometimes twice a week, and occasionally on Saturdays, for a number of years. For two years, I never darkened the door of a grocery store. Peter did the shopping on Saturdays, and I ate whatever was there.

After a while, Peter and I began to talk about relocating. We both loved the mountains and enjoyed nature. An ad appeared in the Sunday *New York Times* describing property here in the Blue Ridge area that sounded as if it could have been written for us. We didn't buy that property, but we fell in love with the area, with its rough mountains and diversity of people. It didn't take us long to find a house, and we have been in this area for fifteen years now. I feel very much at home in these mountains. It's a mysterious kind of feeling, an intuitive feeling of recognition and rightness.

I took some courses in organizational change and became an organizational development consultant for a number of years. This gave me the freedom to take time off to go wherever Peter was working, if I wanted. When he was gone and I was home, I had no other commitments, so I could work on the next consulting assignment.

One assignment was a year in Moorhead, Minnesota, just across the river from Fargo, North Dakota. That was quite a year. There were sixty-three consecutive days when it never got above zero. I discovered yoga while I was there. The wife of the radio station manager started a class in the top-floor storage area of the department store.

Yoga was a life-changing experience for me. I was astounded by some of the things that happened to me in yoga. Very creative things started to come to my mind. I think it was the beginning of looking inside myself for answers instead of outside myself. I began to recapture something important that had been there all along, but had been repressed. It gave me a lot of freedom.

I have changed a lot. As I see it now, my whole life had been a negative pattern. I was always running away from something, leaving something, angry about something, trying to compensate for something, or trying not to be something, instead of moving towards something and developing positive images.

I have only just realized these feelings in the last ten to fifteen years. The amazing part to me, and the part that elicits the most gratitude from me, is that I seem to have been led in the right direction even if I didn't always have the sense to go in it. I always seem to have had an effective antenna for recognizing things that were important to me, that were vital to taking me on to another step.

What I have found at this age is that I think better than I ever did. I remember a time I was reading a book, and I thought, "This is very good writing and I know it's good writing, and I don't have to have anybody else tell me that it is." The awareness that I could think for myself, that I could take facts or situations, and come up with my own conclusions, and feel it was worth something—it was marvelous!

I accepted a position as head librarian at the home office of a large corporation a number of years ago. I think I've done some really significant things for the library. I've set it on a terrific road for the future and accomplished a great deal. It takes a lot of energy to sell what you are doing and convince somebody of it all the time. I think women have had to do too much of that—trying to sell somebody else on our work and the credibility of what we most hold dear.

Now, I feel less and less that I have anything to prove. I would like, soon, to be able to stop working and do just what I want to do for the rest of my life. I'm looking at creative solutions for not working as hard as I have. Maybe that's what life is. Just building it on a daily basis. And learning to let go. A lot of freedom comes with that.

The Women's Room Revisited

Sharon Lester

> I didn't appreciate how important it is to have such pos-
> itive friends until I reached my forties. Maybe we don't
> have the sense to appreciate who anybody is, even our-
> selves, until we gain some wisdom. Someone in the group
> said, "It's a shame you have to be forty years old before
> you start being smart enough to learn how to live."

The women gathered in the family room. Several of them have been friends since grade school. They arrived, one by one, as their busy schedules allowed and wel-comed each other with generous hugs and heartfelt greetings. Each arrived with an offering of food: a casserole, a salad, or a dessert.

Food is an important part of their meetings. It is also a metaphor for the nourishing quality of their relationships. Both tragedy and joy have been served up in generous portions along with the food over the years. The personal stories they have shared have created a strong bond that continues to sustain and inspire each of them.

These friends began to meet regularly when their children started leaving home. They now get together to catch up on each other's busy lives, to provide support for those going through a difficult time, and to celebrate one another's successes and adventures.

One member of this group, Sharon, is a fifty-one-year-old woman in career transition who has been deeply influenced by her friends' positive attitudes and strengths. But they surely have been just as inspired by her story. The loss of her eighteen-year-old sister and her young husband when Sharon was twenty-two taught her that "You could not count on tomorrow."

These early tragedies caused her to focus on the task of raising and educating her sons. By the time she reached forty, her sense of urgency about life prompted her to complete her own education.

This decision energized her, and, as her goal became more apparent, so did the other decisions she needed to make in order to re-create her life on her own terms.

Sharon Lester

I was born in Pennsylvania. Both my parents were schoolteachers. When we moved here to Indiana in the early 1940s, they were unable to teach because the school system did not hire blacks in the secondary school. So my dad went to work at a steel mill, and my mom went to work part-time in the clerical department of a company that made airplane parts. Later, after all the kids were in school, she was able to go back to teaching. By then, they were hiring blacks in secondary schools.

My grandfather and my two uncles were ordained Methodist ministers and educators. My mother taught French, so we learned French when we were growing up.

My home life was fun. We traveled a lot, mostly by car. We visited relatives in major cities: Philadelphia, New York, Chicago, Detroit. My mother is from South Carolina, so we went to the beach on vacation because my family had land there. I remember my dad always took a gun in the trunk of the car when we traveled South. We never stopped after we crossed the Mason-Dixon line—except at filling stations. We didn't spend the night anywhere because there was no place for blacks to stay. When I think back on it, I think how remarkable that was. That in spite of all that, we still traveled.

When I was in my first year of college, my seventeen-year-old sister, Brenda, was diagnosed with acute leukemia. My husband and I were engaged at the time. Brenda wanted to be in our wedding and kept saying, "Please get married soon, or I won't be here to be in the wedding." We were married in June that year. In November, she was dead.

Then, the following July, my husband, James, died in a drowning accident. So I had the opportunity to go through a death experience in the family again. I call it an opportunity because, as I look back, it was such a learning experience.

I learned that tomorrow is not promised to us. It truly is not. Having a sister die at eighteen, and a husband die at twenty-four, I knew you could not count on tomorrow. I think that is why I cram so much into my days now even though I feel extremely stressed from doing it.

After James died, I had to drop out of college to go to work. I had a little baby, and I was pregnant again. I took a job with the phone company, which provided a good income and benefits.

So I worked and raised the boys. They went to Montessori pre-school and to private schools from grade school through college. I thought, "They have to be good, they have to be smart, and they have to be educated." At each step in their education, I thought, "I'll send them to the best school, and, if something happens to me and they can't go further than this, then I'll have given them a good foundation."

The day I took my youngest son off to college, I came home and didn't really notice anything different because the boys were usually gone anyway. That night I turned on the T.V. and watched "Dallas." Then, the next week I did the same, only I had been in the house all week by myself. On Saturday it hit me—I started crying. All of a sudden, it dawned on me that I had watched two episodes of "Dallas" all the way through—no spending Friday nights at the football games, nobody in the house, the kitchen was still clean from the night before. It was such a weird feeling.

It was then I knew there was absolutely no way I could spend my life sitting around crying on Saturday morning. You know, when the kids say, "Get a life?" That's what I did.

Anyhow, after the boys graduated from college, it was my turn to do something with my own life. I went to visit my older son who had moved to California after his graduation. We were sitting around the breakfast table just talking about one thing and another, and I looked around at everybody—my brother-in-law who is a doctor, his sister and my sister-in-law who are teachers, my other sister-in-law who is a medical social worker, and my brother who is a bank vice-president. My son was there, too. Suddenly, I realized I was the only one sitting at that table without a degree. I didn't like what I was feeling.

Going home on the plane, I thought about this awakening I had at the breakfast table. I realized that I didn't feel completed without the college degree. I had taken courses off and on while the kids were growing up. Now I wondered how many credits I would need to graduate.

I didn't go to work the day after I arrived home. I went to the university to find out how many credits I would need and registered right away. After I started, I worked straight through, taking two or three courses at a time. I was determined there was no way I would go back to California and sit around that table again and be the only person without that piece of paper in my hand—without a degree. I was never going to feel that way again.

That promise to myself made a difference in the way I approached my studies. I was driven. I think that drive came from my parents and grandparents. My grandfather was a college graduate. All of my mother's brothers and sisters are college graduates. It was unusual for blacks in the 1930s and 1940s to have that many college graduates in the family. It was just something we did in our family.

Anyway, that experience at the breakfast table was like something inside me saying, "Get off your rear and get started. You don't have a lot of time." I was reminded of what I learned a long time ago—that we aren't promised a lot of time.

My goal was to get my degree, and I did. But then I didn't want to stay at the phone company. I wanted to do something as a professional. I wanted more control over my life, and I wanted to make an impact. So I decided to get a master's degree and teach.

After making that decision, everything else fell into place for me. I owned a big house on property with a lot of grass and trees. My sons were gone, and I decided it didn't make sense to spend my time cutting grass, and shoveling snow, and raking leaves when I needed to invest time in myself. I needed to get focused on finishing my education. I sold my house and bought a condominium.

I began to choose how I would direct my energy. I only had so much of it, so my energy had to go where I wanted it to go. I started to say "no" when my family would ask me to do things. I also began to see that my parents still told me what to do, and that we were too dependent on each other.

When I realized how angry I was about these family things, I went to counseling because I thought something was wrong with me. I learned that I was very healthy to resist the demands and the dependant behavior.

At first, it seemed disrespectful to my parents for me to change. I had always called my mother every day, and, if I could, I would go over there. We got into that habit after my husband died, but that had been twenty years before! It took actual, conscious thought not to call my mother every single day. But a lot of freedom came along with this change.

I don't feel trapped in a job anymore. I took a six-month leave of absence from the phone company, and I will retire at the end of this year. I took a teaching internship at a secondary school. I'll continue teaching for a few years, if I can, to see how I like it. Then, I may continue in graduate school to earn a Ph.D. I'm a month away from my master's degree now. I might like to teach teachers how to teach.

Now, I have choices. I have freedom. I don't have to depend on staying in one job or one city for the rest of my life. I know I can do something with this degree.

I appreciate my education so much. I'm grateful that I stuck with what I wanted to do. Ever grateful! I'm probably a better teacher than I would have been if I had done this in my twenties. I think I understand people more than I would have then.

I'm surprised that life is as exciting as it is at this age. When I was a child, I had schoolteachers who are my age now, and I felt sorry for them. I did not expect life to be this much fun.

I didn't expect to have a boyfriend at this age, and I do. He lives in another town, and I really enjoy him living there. [She laughs heartily.] He's not intrusive or invasive. And, when we're together, we have a lot of fun. I never thought I'd do this much laughing.

I didn't stay stuck. None of my friends have either. When we were raising our kids, we all ran back and forth between each other's houses. As our children went off to college, we began to call each other and say, "Do you want to go to dinner this weekend?" Or, if my sister came to town, I'd call them and say, "She's here. Why don't you come over?"

We had such good times, we continued getting together regularly. We still do. We all look forward to catching up on what each of us has been doing since the last time. These women are so vital! I like being around them because they are so positive.

Everybody is continuing to grow. One woman recently accepted a teaching job at the university for much less money than she was earning, but she loves what she is doing. And she's had opportunities to travel all over—she once spent nine weeks in Mexico. Another woman just had a mastectomy and lost her hair because of chemotherapy. But she is so beautiful!

These are inspiring, spiritual women. I have wondered if it is because we are black women that we feel the need to over-achieve.

You have a family of origin and a family of choice. It's important to be connected to both. What my friends do is very important to me. I like their strength, and their stories are so great. I'm sure my friends did not feel great while they were living through some of them. They were just sort of sad or feeling like they had been kicked in the teeth. But when they tell their stories, everybody knows how they feel. Everybody knows that sick feeling you get when things go badly, and they empathize.

This is the youngest group of fifty-year-old women I know. I think it may be because they all have interesting, active lives. My friend, Betty said, "When my mother retired, she put on a housedress, and suddenly she looked old. I'm not gonna do that." Even though we've been getting together for years, I didn't appreciate how important it is to have such positive friends until I reached my forties. Maybe we don't have the sense to appreciate who anybody is, even ourselves, until we gain some wisdom. Someone in the group said, "It's a shame you have to be forty years old before you start being smart enough to learn how to live."

Forty was a magic number to me—when I began to have that awareness of what I was doing. When you are in your twenties, nursing your babies, changing their diapers—you just do it because it has to be done. I know a woman who said she conceived and gave birth to three human beings—totally unaware. She said she believed she was unconscious during that time.

I'm fifty-one now—a half a century old and having such a good time. I'm tired, but, if I was twenty-five and did the things I'm doing now, I'd be tired. I'm not going to use the excuse that being fifty is making me tired.

Me and the Guy Upstairs

Penny Longworth

> You have to laugh, you have to have a positive attitude,
> too. People can give you advice, but you got to do it.
> You got to do it yourself. They can hold your hand, give
> you a room and feed you, but the bottom line is you got
> to do it yourself. You got to get your mind on doing it,
> doing what you want.

A small garden hugs the side of Penny Longworth's trailer, which is perched on a hillside in rural West Virginia. The garden contains two tomato plants, two pepper plants, and a dirt-smeared tangle of pole beans. Nothing has ripened yet, but the promise is there.

Penny is a generously built woman with curly dark hair. She has such a happily animated face and infectious laugh that it's hard to see her as a victim of both parental and spousal abuse, a high school dropout who has battled poverty all her life.

Only six months before our interview, Penny left her abusive husband of twenty-five years. She had finished raising two daughters and had few hopes for her own future. Although memories of her mother's strength and her own appreciation for nature helped her fight her depression, she came to feel increasingly overwhelmed with thoughts of suicide and murder. As she became more fully aware of these thoughts, she realized that change was imperative for her survival.

With this discovery, Penny decided to seek support from a community program for women in transition. A counselor encouraged her to explore her strengths, and she easily passed the GED. Career testing also confirmed that she is intelligent and talented. This experience lit a spark of self-esteem.

Now, at forty-five, Penny is making plans to attend college. She believes that, having survived years of abuse and poverty, she is equipped to accomplish whatever she sets out to do. She is facing educational, economic and social challenges with a spirit of fun and adventure.

Like her garden, Penny is beginning to bloom.

Penny Longworth

I was born the oldest of eight children. Four boys and four girls. I've always had kids to look after and chickens to chase off the porch and out of my mother's flowers.

We had a farm, and, when dad wasn't working elsewhere, he was working on the farm. He put meat on the table. He used to shoot deer out of season. He didn't care if they was in his fields or someone else's. He outlawed so long that they took his license away from him for life. He just started grinning because he had four boys by then.

My father did teach the love of nature—rabbit tracks and things like that. I was raised in a country setting where you listen to the whippoorwills, and you enjoyed the full moon and the bats flying around. You climbed in the barn overhead. You fell out of the neighbor's plum tree and broke your arm.

We survived. We had a pair of shoes for school, and my dad had steady work pretty much, but I can remember one Christmas when the plant moved to Texas, and he didn't go with it. And there he had eight kids to provide Christmas for. I remember he kept bringing in these boxes. He said Santa got hung up in the lane and told him to bring this stuff on in.

There were clothes and books and stuff. The books had other people's names in them, but we didn't register that. Here one of the guys who was moving to Texas was giving dad stuff he didn't want to take with him, and dad was bringing it home, and it was our Christmas. Those boxes were the greatest things to get into. We found clothes that fit us, like a new sweater. And the storybooks. We'd never had storybooks before.

I learned young to take care of myself and the younger ones because mother was busy. She had a lap child at all times.

We had the pet bunnies and the chickens, but they had to be ate when the time come. We enjoyed walking through the woods and hopping in the swimming hole and catching the frog eggs and watching the tadpoles. We even had our colored peeps one Easter. We raised them and, when they stopped laying eggs, we ate them. When I was seventeen, dad lost the farm, and we moved to Beckley. I was naive back then. I didn't know what boys were good for. I got married when I was nineteen. It was '65. It was my fault we had to get married, not his. I was pregnant. It takes two to tango, but he said it was all my fault.

My father gave me a choice of having the baby and giving it away or marrying the guy. I didn't want to lose my kid, so...

I should have run off. Then I would have been away from my father and my husband. My father expected me to be perfect since I was the oldest of eight kids. If I was a half hour late coming home from the neighbors, I got the belt. He'd strip me down on the bed and whack my ass, my bare skin, with a belt. I'd carry welts. He thought nothing of slugging me around.

Then my husband....it was a vicious chain.

My daughter was born three months after I was married. We had no bathroom and no hot running water. I took all of my clothes to the laundromat every week. I was never allowed to communicate with the neighbors because my husband thought they would put ideas in my head.

I had the second kid in '70, and I wasn't allowed to discipline her at all, not allowed to lick her or anything because she was his pet. I was allowed to raise his oldest one because she had the characteristics of me, so she was my daughter. The one who had his characteristics, he thought, was his daughter.

He was very iron control. If I went to do anything, it was his wishes or not at all. And the grocery list was his; you didn't order parsnips or something he didn't like. He didn't eat them, and you wasn't allowed to buy them.

I took care of my kids, I heated the water on my stove in a galvanized bucket, and I carried it to the livingroom where I put it in a galvanized bathtub and bathed the kids and did what I had to do. And he run around on me for fifteen years and had his girl friends.

Then in '80, I left him temporarily, two weeks, and he put a bathroom and hot running water in for me, so the kids wanted to go back, so I said, okay, I'll go back and try again, but I had lost it. I had turned him off completely mentally. When we were together, I was someplace else. My mind was taking a walk in the woods when I was a kid or—I wasn't there anymore.

I fought back the physical abuse. That was only self-defense, you know. I took a cast iron pan to him one time. He didn't bother me for about three days. Then he was back at it again. Me and the Guy Upstairs got along fine, and my mind wandered off once in a while into pleasanter ideas, and I just managed. You do what you got to do when you got to do it, you know.

There was a lot of sexual abuse, too. The girls don't know about this. He'd bring buddies in, and he'd say—that's when the girls got bigger—and he'd say it's either you or your daughters. So, in order to protect my girls, I....

You do what you have to do at the time. And he had me believing for the longest time that this was the way it was. A woman was supposed to be subject to a man. You wash his head, you do everything he asks. I did have to wash his head, or he went dirty. That's the way his father was, that's the way he was brought up. It's conditioning.

I had to take care of his mother. She was living alone when she first took a spell, and they put her in the hospital. She was a diabetic with a sodium-restricted diet. I had to count milligrams of sodium and all that. Get her up in the morning and get her dressed. Give her her insulin and other medication.

I took care of her from '87 to '90, and I thought, if something happens to her, there's only going to be one person he's going to blame. He blamed me for everything else. Like when he didn't win the lottery, he'd say I jinxed him or witched him. He was very superstitious. He started spending big bucks on the lottery. And he kept blaming me for not having money, for what the kids did wrong, for whatever went wrong.

I was raised to believe the man is the head of the household, but I just felt he was taking over too much of me, and my mind was not going to go. I wouldn't let it. Maybe it was my mother in me. My mother went through a rather abusive life, and she survived it. Her mother had her last baby the day after her father was buried, so my mother had a rough life. Maybe it was something she taught me or something she told me. I don't know.

I got to the point where I was contemplating suicide. I thought about jumping over the banister. Then I got to thinking about how nice that hemlock hedge would look in his Italian seasoning. And then I thought, no, you can't do that. You wouldn't have freedom then. Before I do something stupid, I thought, I'd better get out. I didn't want to end up in solitary some place. And I'd probably mess up suicide and cripple myself, and then I'd really be locked in there. So I left.

I moved out the day after Christmas in '90. I moved out right in front of him. He sat in the staircase and watched me take my stuff out the front door. He said I'd be a bag lady. He said, "You'll never amount to anything, nobody's going to take pity on you, nobody's going to feed you. You're worthless, you don't have no brains, you're not capable of taking care of yourself."

Yeah, I was afraid. But I didn't bring the kids with me this time, they were grown, and that helped. My youngest one told me I deserted her, but she was twenty-one when I left. My other one was married.

It helped to know that welfare was there, that Womenhelp [a community program for women in transition] was there. I went to live with my sister first because Womenhelp has a rule that you have to live away from your husband for two weeks on your own before you can go into a safe house. I have two sisters. One has a husband, and one is a widow. In the daytime, I stayed at the sister's with a husband. When he come home in the night, I'd sleep at the widow's house, so that way I didn't mess up my sister's marriage by moving in. I had my stuff all in her basement, but I wasn't there.

Shirley, my Womenhelp counselor, pretty much put the backbone into my ideas. I knew what I wanted to do, but I wasn't real sure I could accomplish it, and she gave me the confidence that I could do it.

I took my GED test in April of '91, and I passed it. I needed a 225, and I got a 263. I'm a lot freer and happier. I'm able to think and buy what groceries I want to buy, and I've got running water and a bathroom now. [She laughs heartily.]

I did career testing, too. My father and husband had told me that I didn't have a brain, that I was worthless, but the career testing and the GED showed me that I had a brain.

I tested in that career test above ninety in everything but science, and I was above eighty in that. I was just above average in science, and way above average in all the other subjects. Communications and business was my strongest ones. I chose communications. It was like a sixth sense in my life all along, instinct, woman's intuition. I'm headed for college in the fall. I'm happier than a lark right now. I have no problems. Just if my grants for college come through. But when my grants come through, my assistance is going to be shut off and my food stamps. If you go to college, they take it away. If I have a choice of assistance or college, I'd be stupid not to choose college because, on down the road, I can get my bachelor's or my master's. I'll try my bachelor's first, and I'll go from there.

I want to write a novel about my life, and I think I need a little more up here [she points to her head] before I can get it right. I've got the story up there, but I've got to get it out on paper. Maybe I'll start a magazine or my own publishing company or something. What's to stop me? I'm in control.

I wonder how I'm going to get my room and board paid for after September 1, but there's food banks. I'll get a job or something. I'm going to take a civil-service test to be a houseparent at the college. I'm also checking with cerebral palsy to see if they need anybody to stay with someone on a weekend when their regular help is off. I can handle that kind of work. I can cope. I think the Guy Upstairs will take care of me. After what I've been through, He's going to let me starve to death? Get real! [She laughs.]

I'm working on a quilt to sell, too. It's all handmade. I have a sewing machine, but I don't use it. They said I could get a lot for the quilt. I've been at it since the first of the year. I make my own binding, too. If I can get $500 for it, I can buy a car to get around town in.

[She opens up an album on her coffee table. It is filled with pictures of quilts she has made.] That's my granddaughter's baby quilt. I hand appliqued that one. That's a double wedding band quilt. It's all hand pieced and appliqued onto a black sheet. It took me two years to make that. I made one they raffled off for $600 for the high school band. It has musical notes and instruments and the bull dog motto for the school.

Making quilts has always been my escape. I pretty much think quilting was born in me, you know. My grandmother and my great-grandmother were always quilting and putting pieces together. It just seemed to come natural. It was something born in me. I take regular patterns and change them to suit myself.

I don't need a man. I need a degree. I got to write my book. I don't drink, but I go to the club every Friday and Saturday night, and I dance with whoever's there. I'm forty-five and still able to produce, and the thirty-five-year-olds are coming on to me. And I'm saying, get out of my face, boy, I've got plans. I don't need you.

I was about two hundred pounds when I left him. I'm down to 180 now. I thought my shape would turn away the men, but I'm telling you the young ones are coming on to me quicker than the old ones. I was out with a twenty-seven-year-old last night. He took me to his place and cooked me a steak and baked potato with a tossed salad. He taught me how to play pool. He took me back home, and he gave me a nice hug and a peck on the cheek. I love it.

You got to look for the good things in life. Like the little mother bird feeding her babies. You look out your window, and how many shades of green do you see in the woods? How many shades of blue are in the sky in the day? How many times does the moon change its color in a month? It's never the same. You can find beauty if you look for it. You got to look for something.

You have to laugh, you have to have a positive attitude, too. People can give you advice, but you got to do it. You got to do it yourself. They can hold your hand, give you a room and feed you, but the bottom line is you got to do it yourself. You got to get your mind on doing it, doing what you want.

Cherokee Clay

Louise Bigmeat Maney

I am a Cherokee potter.
With my hands I create.
With my mind I create.
With soft clay I create.
As a child I created.
As a young lady my mind drifted.
As I grew older the spirits of creating kept telling me to go back to the old ways.
The spirit became so strong I returned to the old ways.
The art of pottery had never left my mind.
What I learned as a child I never forgot.

Louise Bigmeat Maney (her real name) surrendered in midlife to the identity she had spent most of her life rejecting. She came home to herself as an Indian and as a potter after denying the value of both for over thirty years. When she was a young woman, Louise sought an identity more acceptable to white culture. But an awareness of her heritage was always a presence in her. "It was always in the back of my mind," she repeats like a refrain when she tells her story to us.

Louise's creative process involves her recognition and acceptance of her true identity after a thirty-year period of preparation and incubation. Now, at fifty-nine, Louise is a recognized potter, one of the last of the traditional Cherokee potters. Her work is included in many museums and private collections including the Smithsonian in Washington, D. C. In 1990, she and her sisters had their own exhibit at the Hiestand Hall Gallery at Miami University. Louise's devotion to her Cherokee identity also provides the inspiration for her poetry.

We talk with Louise in her shop, Bigmeat Pottery, in Cherokee, North Carolina. She is a tall and solid woman, shy and soft-spoken. Her dark hair is tied in a bun, and her round, dark eyes look out through tinted glasses. She has an air of quiet confidence, the essence of a woman who has come to terms with who she really is.

The shop is full of distinctive black pots, baskets, beaded jewelry, carved wooden *clan masks, dream catchers, and ceramic pins. Much of the work is Louise's, and all of it is the product of Cherokee craftspersons.*

Pots made by her mother and deceased sister are displayed in a curio cabinet, and photographs of her mother and sister at work are on the wall. She shows us her tools for impressing designs on the clay; they include a polishing stone and a deer's horn, tools her mother and grandmother used.

Louise Bigmeat Maney

I was always close to my mother. I was the youngest in the family, so I stayed with her a lot more than the others did. Growing up, I was happy because I was always home with my mother. All I know I learned from her, more than I learned at school. Like the food we gathered. She would show me what to gather, so I learned all the edible plants. We would pick greens and all kinds of mushrooms and berries. She would tell me what was good for eating and what was used for healing.

The Indian people never used to write anything down. I organized a chart of Indian foods that I made into a poster for the children in the reservation school. I learned about all these things from my mother. We learned to read and write at school, but I learned all my culture from her when I was small.

I can't speak Cherokee. My dad didn't allow it. He didn't want us to be punished for speaking Cherokee like he was when he went to school. But I can understand it when I hear it spoken. I used to sit and listen to him talk to the older Indian people. I would listen hard, and I learned to figure it out. But what my dad said was law, so we just never tried to speak Cherokee.

My dad's dad raised cattle for the Indian people. They lived in seven different clans in those days. One clan would raise meat, one would raise greens, and so on. When the white men came, they couldn't pronounce my family's Cherokee name, so, because he was the butcher (that is what we would call him today), they got to calling my grandfather Bigmeat. The Indians back then only had one name. The whites just gave them a first name and added the name of whatever their vocation was. There's not many Bigmeat's left now.

I told my mother when I was about eight years old that I was never going to make pottery because we had to work so hard at it all the time. We all had to help her. I was about six or seven when I started to help, even younger than that probably. We would have to go and dig all day long in the clay hole. I was small, so I was the one who had to crawl back in the hole and dig out the clay.

The clay bed was three or four miles from our house. My mother and brothers and I would take our lunch and stay there all day and dig out the clay. Then we put it on a sled to haul it home. We would let it dry for three days out in the sun, then beat it into powder and put it in cans with water. Every day we would pour off the dirty water and pour in clean water. It took us two weeks to get enough clay to make pottery. It was hard work.

My mother would trade the pottery she made for food. In the early days, that's the way they did it. There wasn't any money, so we traded what we made for food. We never got paid for anything.

My mother always wanted a little shop, so my dad built her one one summer. Before that, we used to work out under some big maple trees in the yard. We'd sit out there and make pottery. There were hardly any cars back in those days. Whenever a car would come around the bend in the road, we would jump up and run in the house and leave her out there by herself. She would always get mad with us because we would leave her there. We would go in the house and peek out at the tourists. A guide from town used to take tourists out to the houses where Indian people made crafts.

At school, we studied half a day, and we worked half a day. We raised all of the food that we ate in school. We raised potatoes and other vegetables. In the summer, we canned greens and stuff to eat in the winter. We picked berries. We made jam. This is the way I was raised.

After I started to school, I didn't make pottery. There were other things to do. And it seemed like anything Indian was not okay. I didn't want to make pottery because I felt it was not acceptable. You just didn't do Indian things.

When I was older, I learned how to sew, but my mind always wandered to pottery. It was always in the back of my mind. But because I had to work so hard when I was small and because it was Indian, I would never allow the idea to stay in my mind for very long.

When my mother got old, her hands would cramp when she made pottery, so I would help her. I set out the pottery for her, and she would shine it, finish it and design it. I continued to help her for awhile.

I was in my thirties when my mother died. After that, I thought that was the end of pottery for me. I quit when she died. I really missed her because she was just everything to me. After her death, I didn't make any pottery for a long time, but it was still in the back of my mind.

I just stayed home and raised my family. I had seven children. After the children were all in school, I would clean the house, do a little sewing, and, because I didn't have much else to do, I started making pottery again. I was able to sell it and make about $10 a week.

I also decided to go back and finish high school. Back then, if you stayed home and worked, it was considered good. Education didn't mean that much to the Indian people. Work did. When I was in school, college was as far away as the White House is to us here. We just didn't see the importance in education.

After I finished high school, I began to think about working outside the home because, by then, everybody else was working and there I was—just doing pottery at home. My kids enjoyed me being at home when they got off the bus. I would always go meet them down the road and walk with them. But I kept wanting to be out, to be something besides just staying home doing nothing. I didn't go anywhere except church on Sunday. That was it.

I took a job working as an aide at the elementary school on the reservation here even though I really didn't want to work with kids because I did that at home. But I took the job and spent the summers going to college. I took art classes and learned more about pottery. I learned how to throw on a wheel and how to glaze. I taught ceramics for a while. But ceramics is not like molding it out yourself. You are working with somebody else's ideas, so it's just not that pleasing to me to do ceramics.

I never finished college. I jumped from art to art education to middle-school education. I could never decide what I wanted to do, so I continued to work as a teacher's aide for twenty-three years.

When I quit at the school, I was in my forties. I began to work full-time as a potter. I am now doing what I really want to do and had wanted to do all along, but turned my back on when I was younger. Pottery is my main source of life now. I enjoy what I'm doing. I have put myself into being a potter. I have come to the conclusion that it is all I am. This is the only thing I have tried that has worked for me.

To finally know this was a relief to me. I always say now, "I am an Indian, an Indian, an Indian, and that is my life." And what I can do best is pottery. I learned it when I was a small child. That was my gift. Now, if I see something I want to try, I think, "Well, I can do that." Well, I can, and that makes me feel good. When I'm home, I'm either making little faces, little pins, or beads or something from clay. In the evening, I'm never idle. Creating pottery is a part of me.

We bought this property five years ago and converted it into the shop. I have a workshop behind this building. Getting the business started was difficult, but we have come a long way in five years.

I taught my husband how to turn pottery on the wheel. It took him two or three years to learn, and now he turns most of the pottery. I do all of the finish work. I use my mother's tools.

I do some coil pots, but it takes so long, and most people don't want to pay for the time that goes into one. We follow the traditional ways for shining and designing and shaping. We do the traditional firing.

I believe the traditional crafts should be taught in the schools. The basic things like the baskets, the carvings, the pottery. Even if the children may not do it now, later in life the crafts will be there for them.

When I worked at the elementary school, we had to follow the government guidelines, which did not include teaching the Indian culture. But I would take clay over there anyway. We would do beads. I would tell the legends. I always felt I was doing something against the rules. Many of the kids still have the beads and crafts they made. For years, they didn't have any culture in the school. Now they have Indian Culture Week. Just a week to be an Indian.

I belong to the North American Indian Women's Association. I have learned it is this way everywhere, not just with the Cherokee. Every tribe is losing their culture. NAIWA meets once a year to discuss all this and to organize to write congressmen and our tribal leaders about our concerns.

Indian women are more outgoing than they used to be. They used to sit back and take what the men handed down. Now, we get up at meetings and speak if we don't like something that's going on. We're waking up. We have been able to influence change in education and care for the elderly.

If the NAIWAs set out to do something, we get it done. We just don't say we're going to do it. Last year, we started raising funds for a culture center for the children on the reservation, and, by next year, we should have it built.

The children need to be taught their own culture. We learned to be white because that is all they taught us. But I don't think they can ever take the Indian out of us. Our ties are here, and it's hard to break loose from the reservation.

I tried for twenty-three years to get our culture taught in the schools, and now I find that I can do that on the outside. I should have done it years ago. My grandkids, six or eight of them, dance. Two nights a week we get a man to chant with them. I paid him to come and teach my grandkids the traditional Cherokee dances. We put on a show, made all the costumes, and they have really done well. They started when they were six or seven. They are teenagers now and travel all over. Last year, they traveled with the Longhorn Rodeo.

I want to put together dances for the senior citizens. I think they would enjoy moving with the chants of the Cherokee people. I have a tape of the drum and the rattle I'd like to use. Now that I can relax and be what I want to be, there are many things I want to do.

On the Verge

Kathleen Warren

I have continued in this way, just feeling my way around, like a blind person, really, in a strange room. Feeling the texture of things, bumping into stuff, smelling the air...this period now feels very active to me—as if I'm coming alive again and on the verge of something wonderful if I don't push it too much.

Like many women in the forty-to-sixty age bracket, Kathleen Warren is a member of what has become known as the "sandwich generation"—those who juggle caring for their children and for their aging parents. This dual caregiving role is further complicated for midlife women when it involves a conflict of loyalties—loyalty to the emerging self and loyalty to family commitments. The internal demands for personal or professional growth can compete with the external demands of the caregiving role.

This conflict, coupled with the burdens of caregiving, can place women at risk for mental and physical health problems. Taking care of an aging parent often causes unresolved childhood issues and anxieties to surface, and the resulting stress can provoke a true midlife crisis.

Kathleen's story is one many women can relate to. Although maintaining both an academic goal and a family life was a serious challenge, Kathleen found college an affirming experience. Her intellectual skills had not been tested earlier in her life, and her success in college gave her the confidence to set career goals. But Kathleen's time and energies became further divided when her mother became ill with cancer and died.

The next two years were critical. Kathleen had to deal with her own mortality as well as her grief at losing her mother. She also had to wrestle with an overpowering resistance to returning to work that she could not explain. This period of immobilization ended with a surprising resolution.

During a quiet moment one day, the answer to what she was to do next with her life suddenly came to her: She knew she should continue to do nothing. As irrational as the answer seemed, Kathleen's experience was so powerful it could not be dismissed. Intuition told her this was exactly the right direction to take.

The result proved paradoxical. The more Kathleen stopped controlling her life, the more in charge of her life she actually became. As she continued to follow her inner counsel, she discovered her own pace—her own way of being in the world.

Kathleen now feels very alive. She is beginning to work again, but she only selects projects that resonate with her growing sense of herself. Rather than molding her identity from her role, as she did earlier in life, she is now fashioning a role from her re-created self.

Kathleen Warren

My mother was forty years old when I was born. I was an only child. When I was eight years old, my father abandoned my mother and me. He left us without any means of support. My mother had been a homemaker for all her married life, and she didn't have any marketable skills. When my father left, she had a nervous breakdown, and this frightened me a lot. She wasn't able to do much of anything for a while. I don't really remember how long.

After my father left, we found ourselves in a little apartment on the other side of town. My mother tried different jobs to support us, but it was difficult for her to cope with the stress of working outside the home. She tried very hard not to let me know that anything was wrong. But children know when their parents are troubled, so it was confusing to me to hear her say that everything was all right when everything was clearly not all right.

She began taking me into her confidence—talking to me more like a friend than a mother. I began to have trouble concentrating in school. I would get sick in class almost daily and have to come home. I had a lot of anxiety about being separated from her. I felt as if I should be doing something to help her. She did the best she could, but there wasn't enough income. I didn't know what I could do about that. I was scared.

When I was about eleven or twelve, she remarried and our lives stabilized. My life became pretty normal. I had the usual adolescent traumas, but, all in all, I enjoyed being a teenager in the '50s. Because my mother was remarried, I felt I could be on my own and enjoy these years. I had a secure home, and she had a happy marriage.

I married in my early twenties, and my husband and I started a family almost immediately. We had two daughters in four years. I settled into the same life as all my friends. In the meantime, my stepfather retired, and he and my mother moved to Colorado where he had a ranch he had inherited.

It was quite a lifestyle change for my mother but a real adventure. They came back to Missouri every summer for month-long visits.

It seemed to me that she and I had moved forward into a mature mother-daughter relationship. During these years, we became a touchstone for each other about what we had been thinking, particularly regarding each of our spiritual lives. She was alone much of the time on that ranch, and it gave her a lot of opportunity to think and develop her own insights. I had my own as well, and we would share these during her visits.

When my stepfather died suddenly, my mother moved back to Springfield. At the beginning, she did well. She was eighty years old then, and I felt that she was really hitting her stride. She had a little apartment she furnished with only the furniture that she wanted. For the first time in her life, she didn't have to compromise or please anybody except herself. She also began to make some friends of her own. She took walks, went to the library, joined a singing group. She was pretty independent.

I would take her out to lunch and to buy groceries once a week. She would often come to dinner on Sunday. The level of my responsibility was pretty comfortable. I was enjoying our relationship.

By this time, I had adolescent daughters and a marriage that, after surviving some stressful times, had become overall very stable. I had been attending some leadership training events at my church and discovered I had some skills in this area. That gave me new confidence. My husband urged me to go to college. I had always wanted to, and now I thought I might want to teach.

I was forty by then. Sometime in my thirties, I began to feel somehow that I had lost my own sense of identity. Something important was missing. I didn't know what it was, I just knew I was unhappy. But that period of my life brought me to the decision to get a college degree. I wasn't sure I could manage it. Once I started classes, though, I completely enjoyed the challenge.

I was three years into my undergraduate degree when my mother was diagnosed with cancer. During the next five years, she became increasingly dependent. I was in school full-time, taking care of my family, and now my mother needed care on a daily basis—cooking, cleaning, all the financial stuff. I took her to chemotherapy treatments and doctors' appointments. She was ill from the treatments for most of the first year. She also became clinically depressed and eventually even had shock treatments.

I remember feeling confused about wanting to do it all—stay in school, take care of her, and take care of my family. I also felt a little resentful. I didn't want to drop out of school. I was very much aware of my age and felt like time was running out if I wanted to complete the degree and work in my field.

As time went on, I became more and more compulsive about managing her affairs and being the best student possible. I think what was happening was that her frailty and dependency threw me back into my own childhood feelings of helplessness and anxiety. I felt that I had to keep doing something, stay in control, or she would get worse, and I would be responsible. I thought, if I just worked at it hard enough, she would get better.

So I spent a great deal of time talking on the phone to doctors—sometimes calling from a phonebooth between classes. The year she had chemotherapy I would often go from a class to the hospital, back to an afternoon class, then home to prepare dinner. I'd deal with the girls' problems, feed everyone, and then go back to the hospital. And, of course, there was library research and papers to write.

The year before I graduated, I went into therapy. I had been taking too much Valium, and that worried me, and, more and more, the Valium wasn't taking care of the anxiety. The therapy helped me stop taking the Valium, but I still couldn't seem to stop taking charge of everything.

As my mother became more frail, I got more and more frantic about questioning the doctors. One day I had a long list of questions about her medication, and her doctor just began yelling at me. He must have been very frustrated with me. But I thought I had to do everything I could on her behalf.

After I graduated, I accepted a job as a legislative aide. But then I began to have health problems. I finally had to have a hysterectomy. During my convalescence, I watched a lot of videos and television even during the day. Just numbing out. I remember feeling so helpless—just very, very helpless—because I couldn't change my mother's situation.

I think I felt more love for her in those years than I ever had before. As I finally began to accept the inevitable, my energies went more toward making her comfortable. Sometimes I would bring her a cup of coffee, and just hearing her say, "Oh, that tastes so good to me," would fill me with such satisfaction—that she could at least experience some small pleasure.

But I often felt a real impatience with her, too. I hope she was never aware of it. I used to think if she would only try harder she could at least gain some control over her life. She was clinically depressed, and I didn't know how to deal with it. I just couldn't accept it.

By the end, she had suffered a great deal. One day in the hospital, she looked at me and asked, "Why does there have to be so much suffering?" It broke my heart. It was all very, very sad.

I wasn't with her when she died, and I very much regret that. I had become so exhausted and anxious that I couldn't stay with her for long periods. When she became comatose, I would kiss her "hello" and touch her, then sit with her, but I couldn't speak to her like the nurses encouraged me to do. I felt paralyzed at the end, and it still grieves me that I didn't let her know enough that I was with her.

After she died, I felt wounded, as if a part of me had been ripped away. I missed her very much, and I was so aware of how much I had loved her. I was surprised by this grief because I only expected to feel relieved that her suffering was finally over.

I think I just shut down after that. I quit my job and went on an extended vacation with my husband. When we returned home, I just puttered around the house. I watched soaps, went to dinner with friends, read a lot of books. This went on for two years. I became bored, but I had lost interest in the idea of going back to work. I tried several volunteer jobs, thinking I could jump-start myself, but I didn't seem to fit into anything. And I was burned out from caregiving roles.

As time went on, I became pretty morbid about my own death. I really came face to face with my own mortality. I experienced a long period of deadness—a lack of feeling and energy. And I'm only beginning to be able to let go of this sense that I failed my mother in some way, that I didn't do everything I could have for her.

The experience with my mother made me realize I needed to learn to let go, to give up some control so that I can accept my own death when it is time. I would like to be able to die well, but, more importantly, I want to live well—with more grace and ease. I have given this a great deal of thought since she died.

Over and over, I tried to put pressure on myself to go back to work to get out of this black mood and to stop the grieving. But there was an incredible resistance in me. I felt stuck. I had no idea what I wanted to do next.

Gradually, I began to trust this inactivity. Where this trust came from, I don't really know. But every time I would consider looking for a job or think about starting a little business or some project, an alarm would go off inside me like a warning. At first, I thought it was anxiety.

A turning point occurred one day when I was doing my yoga. The house was very quiet, and my mind was still. I had been worrying about what I was going to do with my life. Something very clear inside me said I should do nothing. Just wait. I was completely startled by the idea that doing nothing might be an answer to my stuckness. It seemed too outrageous. But the feeling was just so pervasive that I couldn't ignore it. I didn't know where this would lead, but I was certain it was right for me.

So I just began doing things that gave me pleasure. For example, I would browse in the bookstore and buy books strictly by intuition. I mean, I wouldn't think about whether this book would be good for me to read or even if it was interesting. I would buy it if reading the table of contents or jacket cover made me feel good.

Something else I did was to decide that, since I was already alone much of the time, rather than continue to try to find ways to be with someone, I would see if I could enjoy my own company again. My life had been so crowded with people and things in the past twenty-something years. It worked. I began to enjoy rather than fight against my isolation.

Of course, there were many times that all of this seemed self-indulgent to me. That was when I would begin to plow through the want ads looking for an job. But whenever I came across something that seemed somewhat interesting, something that I might consider, that inner alarm would go off.

I have continued in this way, just feeling my way around, like a blind person, really, in a strange room. Feeling the texture of things, bumping into stuff, smelling the air. I'm sure it appears to others as if I'm still not doing anything. But this period now feels very active to me—as if I'm coming alive again and on the verge of something wonderful if I don't push it too much.

I've started writing some poetry. I used to write a journal years ago. Now I'm writing a little, nothing serious—just little poems about my observations and memories.

I've also been asked by a consultant friend who's a lobbyist to work with her on a project. I'm going to do it. I have the skills for it, and it's a project I can do without getting drained. I'm ready to work at something short-term. I seem to be resurrecting old talents. I just realized that as I'm saying it.

I'm fifty now. I feel like I have taken on a great deal in this past decade. Now I would like to enjoy life more, create new relationships with my grown daughters and my husband. I'm looking forward to some satisfying work. I feel certain that something interesting and vital is just ahead for me.

A Good Italian Girl

Virginia Marino

> Something about turning 40....gave me the freedom to
> say, "I don't care as much about what other people think.
> I don't have to prove anything to anybody anymore.
> I've proved it to myself. I'm comfortable with myself."

*Virginia Marino, forty-seven, invites us into her home just a few days after she has
returned from a vacation to Italy, the country that her father's family left a generation ago to come to America. She shows us her souvenirs—prints, festival masks,
Murano glass objects, her grandmother's birth certificate. It's clear that Virginia's
vacation has given her a special appreciation of her Italian heritage.*

*Growing up in an Italian-American family was a very intense experience.
Virginia's father believed he should have absolute control over his children, which
included making decisions for them. He also demanded that they be perfect—in
school, in appearance, in social situations.*

*By the time Virginia was eighteen, she was overwhelmed by a lack of self-knowl-
edge, low self-esteem, and an inability to make decisions. Her history as a young
adult seesawed between attempts to rebel and attempts to prove her worthiness.*

*Moving to another city in her mid-twenties gave Virginia the freedom she felt
she needed to build an identity of her own. Over the next fifteen or so years, as she
began to realize her strengths, she started to acquire some perspective on her childhood. Unfortunately, to some degree, she also allowed her career to become a
source of security, and she became the dutiful employee continually striving to
prove herself. A severe, chronic case of hives finally forced her to deal with the
stresses she had allowed to accumulate.*

*As she approached forty, Virginia felt it was time to assess her life and to make
some changes. Realizing that she was comfortable with herself allowed her to make
the decision to return to her hometown. Five months later, she began a caring
relationship with a man she has since married. A year after she returned home, she
also entered a graduate program in preventive medicine, a field that has opened up
exciting research possibilities for her.*

Reaching midlife has given Virginia an important freedom. After years of strug-gling to please her father, husband, employers, and lovers, she knows that the only person she needs to please is herself. And that's just what she is doing.

Virginia Marino

I was born in New Jersey. Growing up was not real good. My parents should have never gotten married to each other. Although I'm sure they loved each other very much, they were not very compatible.

Mom started dying when I was fifteen and ended up dying when I was nineteen and in my freshman year at college. She had ovarian cancer. She was forty-five. Her illness was the family secret. We weren't allowed to tell anybody about it because people believed cancer could possibly be conta-gious. It was 1966. We lived in a town of thirty-five thousand people, those were the kinds of beliefs they had, maybe not that the general public had, but they were certainly the beliefs that my father and mother held. So I was sworn to secrecy.

Her illness was very painful to us, and there was nobody to talk to about it. My dad was in a very bad state. He didn't know what to do. It was out of his control, and that was very frustrating for him. There were two of us kids, and he didn't know what to do with us. Mom just kept wasting away.

When I went away to college, I didn't know how to behave because I'd never made a decision for myself in my whole life. So I made a lot of very bad decisions very quickly.

Good Italian girls didn't make decisions. Their fathers made all their decisions for them. You didn't question, and you didn't dare disobey, or you would be pounded to within an inch of your life. My father literally decided what time I would go to bed, what time I would get up, what I would wear, what clothes were purchased for me, what activities I took part in at school, who my friends were, everything.

Anyway, at college, I did lots of alcohol and lots of drugs. I had sex with...not a lot of people. I guess I didn't have an opportunity to make too many bad decisions in college because my mom died in February of my fresh-man year.

When I went back to school after her funeral, I was really psychologi-cally distressed. But no one thought of counseling or any kind of support for a kid whose mother had died. I set the trash on fire in my trash can. It seemed like a good idea at the time. The whole dorm room filled up with smoke and set off all the smoke detectors. They decided I better go get some counseling. I was probably angry and upset, acting out my feelings.

Then that summer, I went home to live with my dad and my brother. I was seeing somebody and would stay out late. My dad got me a job, but I quit it because I couldn't stand it. For a couple of days, I pretended I was going to work, but he found out.

He beat me with a belt. I turned black and blue. Then the next day, he looked at me with bruises from here to there and asked me what happened. "Oh, you beat me with a belt last night in an absolute rage because I lied to you." Anyway, yeah, I guess I was home that summer.

I went back to school in the fall. I started hanging out with the drug crowd again. I met a motorcycle biker type of fellow. I really was not doing well at all psychologically because of my mom. I went out with him for a while, and I got pregnant. So he was going to try to find a way to get me an abortion through his friend.

That didn't work out, and I was getting increasingly frantic because I had no idea what I was going to do. I believed my father truly would kill me this time.

I remember my father was hung up about anything remotely sexual, like if I threw away an empty box of Tampax, he got upset because my brother might see it in the garbage can. I don't know what was supposed to happen—would he ask what a Tampax was? Then what would happen? Would the world end?

So I went to California with a girlfriend and had the baby, a little girl. I put her up for adoption. Giving up the baby wasn't easy. She was in foster care for a while, and I visited with her, and I agonized over her. The fellow who got me pregnant was either killed or committed suicide when I was five months pregnant. Not that I would have married him. I should have never gotten involved with him in the first place.

Then I re-established contact with my dad. I didn't tell him I had been pregnant, but my girlfriend told him. Bad time. Bad time. It was okay for me to come home as long as I didn't ever tell anyone what had happened. No one was to know about this horrible sin.

I went back to college and pretty much straightened up. I went to therapy at the university's counseling center. I decided I would become a social worker. The social worker at the adoption agency in California was the first functional female role model I think I had run into in my life. She was doing something interesting, and she had a life of her own, and she had empathy and was willing to talk to me. She treated me with some respect. I was allowed to make decisions and have input about what happened.

Anyhow, I got a degree in social work. Got married at the end of my senior year. Got pregnant a year after that. Got divorced two years after that.

I got married because I was graduating from college, and I had no other idea what I was supposed to do. I didn't even know you had to figure out what to do. I just figured I knew what to do: You got married. That's what you did. You had a college degree and all that, but you might use it, and you might not use it. In terms of making any plans or thinking about how I wanted to live my life, I didn't have any real rational thought processes. Most things were kind of impulsive, kind of intuitive, and I just did them.

I got married to somebody I thought would take care of me, parent me. Of course, he was looking for me to take care of him. You know how that goes. It didn't work out. I was twenty-four years old. I thought, "Why am I married? What am I doing here? What is the point?" I was really, really lonely.

After my divorce, I figured that I would get married again right away. Because what else was I supposed to do? I had a two-year-old. I started dating somebody who was older. He had money, he was romantic, he was sexually functional. He took me to Spain. I really, really thought I was in love with him. He just sort of dumped me after I'd been going out with him for about seven or eight months.

I had never really grieved for my marriage being over, but, when Don dumped me, then it really hit me. "Oh, my God, I have a two-year-old daughter, I'm totally alone, I don't have any money, I'm living in public housing." I joked about being downwardly mobile after the divorce. I had a job as a social worker, and I made about $8,000, so we still qualified for subsidized housing. I was so overwhelmed. I wondered what on earth I would do with my life. I got promoted at work and moved out of public housing. I had affairs with different people. I kept thinking that a relationship would work out, and I would get married.

I spent my time trying to be what the men I dated wanted me to be. I never even thought about what I wanted to be, or what I wanted them to be because I was so busy trying to meet their expectations. I kept striving to be better, so maybe they would love me, and then maybe I would feel okay, and I would love me, too, and we would all be happy. That didn't happen.

I remember one time I went home for a wedding or family reunion or something. I might have been twenty-eight by this point. My uncle took me aside and said, "You know you are never going to get married again. Nobody is ever going to want you now. You're too old and you've been married before and you have a child." I thought, "You son of a bitch, this is just what I need to hear." But it just reinforced what I was starting to believe at this point.

I decided I didn't want to do social work anymore. Social work made me feel guilty because I never felt like I was doing enough for people, and I couldn't put any distance between myself and them.

I quit the agency and studied to get my FCC license. I was a disc jockey for a while at a little radio station and at two discotheques in the evening. I got to dress up and go out late at night and spin records. I was also a bartender for awhile, and I was in sales, too. I was floundering around.

I heard about a federal job opening up that involved working with women who had pelvic inflammatory disease. I interviewed and got the job. I had to relocate to another part of the country, but the job had a career ladder, and it was a great opportunity. I thought, "I can leave town, and I can start all over again."

I felt that I couldn't change there in my hometown. There were too many expectations of me to stay who and how I was, and I didn't want to do that anymore. I wanted to try to be healthier, stronger, stop being such a weeny, I guess.

Anyway, I moved to Baltimore. The clinic was really kind of fascinating and my co-workers were okay. I felt proud of myself. I started getting promoted, and I felt like maybe I was competent.

My father was appalled by my moving to Baltimore. At this point, I was starting to realize that he wouldn't be happy no matter what I did. So I said, "I'm going to do what I want to do, or at least what I think I want to do since I don't know what I want to do because I don't trust my ability to make decisions." But my intuition on going to Baltimore was the right thing to do.

It helped me to start putting my relationship with my father into perspective.

During that period of time, I started running. Running made me feel really good, really strong. I could run a ten-kilometer race, I could run a ten-mile race, I could do that. I was starting to think in terms of having some kind of goal other than getting married to be rescued.

It was a good idea to go to Baltimore. Good idea. In some sense, though, I felt I had substituted my career for a marriage. My career was my security now. I felt that the agency would take care of me. If I tried hard at work and got a gold star on my evaluations, they would give me a raise, and I could get some gratification from using my mind.

I got promoted again to a supervisor position, which meant a move to upstate New York. I had a staff and all the stresses involved with directing the staff. I was traveling for my job. I bought an old house, so I was somewhat strapped for money and had to worry about making repairs on the house.

I also got involved with an attorney in Washington who I just adored. He was the man of my dreams, my prince. Good-looking, funny. He was so attentive, he did things for me, like he ironed my clothes. We would fly every other weekend back and forth, and we would talk long distance on the phone almost every night, and we would write letters to one another.

Well, those things don't last, but I didn't realize that at the time. I was thirty-six by then. The traveling and the distance started to wear on our relationship after a couple of years.

I remember that Christmas holiday. I was getting ready to go to my father's home in Jersey, and, when I woke up one morning, I was covered with hives, big welts on my face. At first, I thought I must have eaten something bad or developed an allergic reaction to something. I flew home anyway.

The hives became the size of oranges. My eyes were swollen shut, and my lips were swollen, and they itched terribly. I had to go to the emergency room and get intravenous cortisone. They were afraid I was going to get the hives in my throat, which can asphyxiate you. I was very, very distressed.

When I got back to New York, I couldn't work. The doctors put me on steroids, which are horrible, and I gained twenty pounds in three weeks. My heart was pounding all the time. Nobody could figure out what was causing the hives. Some people suggested stress, which was certainly a reasonable suggestion considering all that was going on.

When Ken saw me for the first time with hives, he freaked out. He was attentive as long as I looked right and behaved right. But I wasn't looking right, and I wasn't behaving right, and I was in a very bad way.

Steroids can make you kind of psychotic. I was also taking all these other anti-inflammatory and antihistamine drugs to keep the hives under control. I was slurring my words and having trouble keeping awake. I'd been taken over by this chronic disease.

Gradually, through therapy and ending the relationship with Ken and getting a promotion to a rural part of New Hampshire, I got myself straightened out. I went to Weight Watchers and dropped the twenty-five pounds. I got the hives under control. I bought a house I liked a lot better than the one in New York. I became very functional.

I was about to turn forty, and I thought it was time to reassess. Here I was, the head of a program, but I hated being an administrator, I hated supervising people. I was sick of public health, I was sick of sexually transmitted diseases. I knew that what I had to look forward to every few years was another transfer someplace else and another transfer after that.

I remembered Ken saying to me, "How can you realistically expect to have a relationship with somebody when you are consumed by your career and every two years you are going to get transferred? Who is going to follow you around the country?" I remember thinking, "Well, I really want a relationship and a career. Why can't I have both of them? Why do I have to choose one or the other? When do I ever get to exercise all parts of myself? Why can't I be intellectually satisfied and emotionally satisfied?"

I sent a letter of resignation to the agency. I told them I didn't think being transferred every couple of years was good for me. But they asked me not to resign, and they found me a job in New Jersey because I told them I wanted to move back home.

Turning forty said something to me like, "If you want to go home, you can. You won't be the same person you were when you left. People won't define you anymore. You can go back there and be whoever you want to be." So I did.

Something about turning forty also gave me the freedom to say, "I don't care as much about what other people think. I don't have to prove anything to anybody anymore. I've proved it to myself. I'm comfortable with myself."

After I had been back in Jersey for about five months, my friend Judy introduced me to this guy named Paul. I thought, "Judy, this guy is so dull and so boring, and he is not interested in me, and I am not interested in him, and I don't know what we are doing here." But three weeks later, a jazz group came to town that I wanted to see. I broke down and asked Paul to go, and we had a good time. So we went from there.

But I did so many things differently. I didn't have sex with him for quite a while, and, before I had sex with him, I made him tell me his sexual history. That is something I wouldn't have done before because I wouldn't have thought I had a right to do it. I would have just let things happen. Not anymore.

I said, "If I am going to have sex with you, I want to know if this relationship is going to continue, and I want to know what your intentions are." He was quite taken aback. I thought, "I am worth something here, and I am protecting myself and being realistic." I was forty-one when we met.

We did embark on a more intimate relationship. And after a year or so, he moved in, and we lived together for three years. We bought a house together. Then, last summer, we decided that we should be married.

But I didn't get married to be rescued. I got married because I love him and want to spend my life with him and accept him. This is probably the first adult relationship I have had in my whole life with a man.

My father actually gave me away at the wedding. My relationship with him had gotten better after I refused to see him for about five years. We approached one another gradually and tried to treat each other with respect and some degree of understanding, to not play the old scripts over and over again.

During the same time Paul and I were living together, I decided to take a leave of absence from the agency to go back and get a graduate degree in preventive medicine because I became interested in science, in analysis, things that I was never interested in when I was younger.

Now I'm in graduate school, and I'm really interested in breast cancer research. My mother died of ovarian cancer. I am going through midlife. When I get through menopause, should I take estrogen or shouldn't I? What risks does estrogen therapy pose? It really hasn't been studied. I want to be a part of that research. Maybe I can contribute to a body of knowledge that will benefit both me and all women to some extent.

I think it took me a long time to get where I am now. One of the things I can do, one of the things I have tried to do, is to be a better mother to my daughter, to help her make her own decisions. I want to give her room to grow and to express herself, to develop better feelings about herself, so she can make this journey in a shorter period of time. Then life will be even better for her daughter. Each generation will grow a bit further.

Inn-Ward Journey

Anne Castle

> This change in my health requires me to enjoy life in
> the moment rather than in long-range goals. I don't know
> how long I have to live. Living here is important to me
> now. These hills are the face of God to me.

*"The most powerful transitions of my life have been occurring since I became
forty," Anne says, extolling the virtues of midlife. "A favorite quote of mine describing spiritual transformation is 'My soul came forth like an avalanche and the face of
my mountain would never be the same again.' This describes my experience as well."*

*Like a mountain, Anne Castle (her real name) has been profoundly affected
by an interior movement. She has changed from an outer-directed, goal-oriented
person to one who takes her cues about life from deep within herself. This creative
shift in focus has affected every facet of her life. Her recognition of a spiritual
dimension required change in her marital status, her vocation, her perception of
herself, and in her belief in the existence of God.*

*Braving the territory of an inward journey takes a particular courage, and
Anne's journey had life-altering implications.*

*It's a rainy winter evening. The inn that Anne founded hugs the roadside deep
in the Hocking Hills of Southern Ohio. Inside, the enticing smells of dinner prepa-
rations make a delicious backdrop to our conversation. Anne tells us how important
it is to learn to live in the moment and how old habits of thought interfere with living
fully in the present.*

*At fifty-seven, Anne is a small, intense woman with radiant white hair and
dark eyes. Her manner is clearly focused and suggests a state of readiness. Perhaps
this is because Anne is being challenged on several levels: physically, vocationally
and spiritually.*

*The inn's peaceful, rural setting is a world apart from the affluent and ambi-
tious existence Anne has abandoned. She recalls her years as a corporate consultant
and the events that led her to begin an intense inward journey.*

Anne Castle

My image in those days included a shocking pink ultrasuede suit with designer shoes. I had an impeccable hairdo, was impeccably groomed, living an impeccable life. I remember toward the end of that period getting on a plane to do a consulting job for the University of Alabama. My daughter, who was seeing me off, said, "You know, Mom, you have realized your dream. You've made it!"

All the time I was on that trip, I thought, "She's right." I was, in that moment, everything anybody ever wanted to be. I had really made it. But in the back of my mind, I wondered, "Where am I going now?"

At this point, our family was in counseling. I had not consciously been thinking about divorce even though there were enormous problems in the marriage.

One day I was sitting in the garden and studying (by then, I had begun my master's work). Suddenly, a quiet voice inside me said, "If you don't leave this marriage, you will never grow further." I began to cry. I realized it was true.

Until then, I had no spiritual life. If you had asked me then, I would have told you I was agnostic, maybe even an atheist. So I knew something important was happening. And the decision to divorce was exactly the right decision.

I started learning meditation from a wonderful teacher who began to talk to me about a Higher Self. I didn't know if I believed in that. But one morning, I woke up crying. Joyful crying. I shot up in bed, saying, "Oh, my God. There is a God!" And I knew that in my gut. Again, it was that clear voice within me.

After that, I needed to be on my own for a while. I decided to discontinue the consulting altogether. The divorce was not yet final and had become a very ugly experience. I awoke one day and knew I was going to buy a van and leave Columbus. By now, I was learning that I should accept these experiences and act on them.

It is hard for me to describe how I am so sure of that voice inside except to say I can hear it with my whole body. It really touches me to the core, and I know it's my Higher Power speaking. It is a very spiritual, joyful experience, which I respond to with tears.

When I began to price vans, everybody thought I had gone over the edge. I took off in my van and traveled for six months up and down the East Coast. I picked up consulting jobs to earn my way. During a camping trip in the Blue Ridge Mountains, I was eating breakfast in a restaurant and had a strong sense that I was never going to live in the city again. I just knew I had to live in the hills.

I looked up at the waitress and thought, "I don't care if I have to wait tables, but I have to live in the hills." I wanted to be surrounded by nature. I knew that is where I would find oneness with God.

It is difficult to explain how the idea of the inn developed. It was somewhat like my decision about the divorce except I had learned so much more about myself that the process was more conscious.

After considering several locations, I decided I wanted to live in the Hocking Hills. I used to visit a friend here during difficult periods of my life, and I came to love this place. The idea of the inn developed out of knowing where and how I wanted to live.

At the time I began to look at property, I was really low in capital. I thought this one hundred acres was too much land even though I became certain this was the right piece of property. It included a broken-down old house with no furnace and several outbuildings.

When I moved here, I had no money at all. My first winter without a furnace, I got up every night to stoke the fire in the fireplace. In the summer, I slept on the front porch. Everybody had thought I was crazy to go off in my van. Now they thought I was really crazy. But I had a few friends who understood my dream and believed in what I was doing. They loaned me the money to make the down payment.

In the end, many people became involved. We were able to secure shareholders, and others were influential in working through rough complex financial blocks. I had a friend, a bank officer, who got me a loan past every obstacle. Other than his believing in this dream, there was no other reason the loan should have cleared. Nothing was right. Everything was wrong with the property in terms of securing the loan.

I believe that all the resources for this dream of the inn to become a reality were in place all along. When things looked bleak financially, someone would turn up wanting to buy some shares. When securing the loan to build the guest lodge seemed hopeless, a friend turned up who knew the bank president, and the loan was cleared. [Her eyes well up with tears.]

The mission of the inn is to bring people from the cities out here to this very special land to expose them to nature, to provide an experience of nature so that people will learn to love the earth.

The first big weekend we had, I was up early taking my walk up the hill, and I looked down at the inn and thought, "This is exactly the way I visualized it. Exactly!" It is mind boggling to me that these things are possible. I now believe there are no limits except those we put on ourselves; as long as it is for our own good and the good of others, we can realize our dreams.

A newspaper reporter came to interview me for a feature article about the inn, and, at the end of the interview, I told her I was feeling uncertain about telling her about the spiritual aspect of all this. I didn't want to scare people off. She smiled at me and said, "Anne, you said what all this was about was trust. Why did you think I would be different from any of the others? Just trust."

That article had an impact on a phenomenal number of people. The next week hundreds of people poured into the inn. Many of them would probably never stay here—they just wanted to shake my hand. People responded to the idea of someone who had nothing to start with but a dream.

Now I've been diagnosed with cancer. Even if the tumor, which is gone now, stays away, they will never be able to tell me I'm healed. This change in my health requires me to enjoy life in the moment rather than in long-range goals. I don't know how long I have to live. Living here is what is important to me now. These hills are the face of God to me.

I know that to develop spiritually is enough. That is what those of us who are involved in this direction are doing for the world. Solitude connects us with nature and, as our spiritual life changes, we become part of something universal.

The whole of Anne's midlife has been characterized by change. She allowed herself to risk in order to live a more expanded life. She believed that death was yet another stage of growth not to be feared.

Anne died in August, 1991. Until her death, she continued meditation and healing, which allowed her to deal with the pain and to remain aware. Four days before her death, she was able to hike in her beloved hills with her daughter, Ellen.

In her journal, Anne kept a daily record of her process of relinquishing her attachments to the inn and to her family and friends. A favorite quotation of Anne's by Charles DuBois from The God Within *summarizes the way she lived and died: "In order to grow we must be willing to leave all that we have ever been to become all that we could be."*

A Sure Touch

Nena Berger

> Life is becoming more simple for me. I am becoming
> more quiet and more creative. As a child, I was such a
> hold- still, good little girl. Now I am enjoying move-
> ment, such as T'ai Chi and dance....I am more open to
> following something that might catch my interest.

*It is a cold, rainy day as we hurry through the busy city streets toward the art deco
office building. When we enter the Massage Center office, the calming scents of
massage oils and herbal teas welcome us like a nurturing mother. The room is
warm and light even on a cloudy day. Ivy plants thrive in the window.*

*We are greeted by Nena, a charming forty-nine-year-old woman recovering
from alcoholism and workaholism. She is a massage therapist—a career she chose
after getting into recovery when she was forty-four. She is a petite woman with well
defined, delicate features. Although her short, reddish-brown hair and freckles give
her a Peter Pan quality, she projects a quiet strength and serenity.*

*Nena tells us her story as we warm ourselves with cups of herbal tea. She
describes her childhood isolation and the destructive effect it had on the way she
valued herself. As an adult, she could only measure her worth in terms of her work.*

*In her mid-forties, Nena began her own recovery process—a process that has
eased her frantic pace and allowed her time to discover who she is apart from work
and alcohol dependence.*

*Nena has a fresh career that evolved naturally from her recovery experience.
Her new work as a massage therapist has provided an opportunity for her to tap
into her creativity. The images that come to Nena these days have powerful implications for her life in recovery. They are images of strength, clarity, and wisdom.*

Nena Berger

My mother was suicidal when I was born. I had an older brother who was stillborn. Eleven months later she had me, and eleven months after I was born, she had my younger brother. My mother never recovered from the loss of my older brother and was never emotionally available to me.

My father was a workaholic—a good German, you know? The typical patriarchal type of man. He believed in hard work. He thought that, if he supported the family, he had done his due. I do remember him as being a real sensitive man, though, on the few occasions he was with me. He was seldom home. There was really no one at home.

So before the age of five, I spent lots of time outside in the woods. I feel as though I was raised by nature because that's where I hung out—interacting with trees, plants, water.

When I was five, my mother began taking in foster infants to care for. Over the years, she took in a hundred infants. That made her even less available to me. In a book I wrote about workaholism, I refer to my parents as "ghost parents": I could see them, but I couldn't feel them. I was very happy when I got into school. It was wonderful to have contact with people.

When I was twelve years old, I was molested by a great-uncle. In the two years that followed, he sexually harassed me constantly in front of my parents and my aunt. And they never said anything about it.

Later, when I was in my thirties, I began to suspect that my mother had been sexually abused by the same uncle. When I asked her about it, she giggled and said, "Oh, he got you, too?" I thought, "This is my mother?" After that, I was very angry at her for having sent me to my uncle's house as a child—knowing he was a sexual abuser.

When I was fourteen, I became engaged to an older boy who joined the Navy. I am appalled that my parents let me do that. But the engagement protected me from having to face or deal with any sexual experiences. So I became a very good student. I broke the engagement when I was eighteen and decided to go to college.

As a result of these experiences in my childhood, I had no models for being in a family—or for just being a person, you know? I thought that working was how you became someone.

I had an aunt who was very supportive and encouraged me to go on to college. She was a physician, and I admired her very much. She told me I could do whatever I wanted to do. My parents thought I should get married and have babies. At that time, a woman had few choices. You were either a nurse, a teacher, or you had a family. I chose teaching.

I met my husband while I was in college. I didn't know it then, but he was an alcoholic. He taught me how to drink hard liquor. Even then, I noticed how unpredictable my behavior was when I drank. After the first couple of swallows, I couldn't control what I did, and I became very promiscuous.

I became very ill the first time I drank alcohol. I had dry heaves and other hangover symptoms for days. Of course, I vowed I would never drink hard liquor again. I drank beer throughout college even though I didn't like it. These were clues that something was wrong, but I ignored them.

After I graduated, I moved to the town where my husband was living. I proposed to him, and we got married. I taught high school for awhile. It was while I was teaching that I first began to show signs of workaholic behavior. I was extremely compulsive. I invented it!

The schools now would be delighted to have me because each child I taught had a personal learning plan. This took up all my time at night. Of course, I didn't have much of a relationship with my husband. I didn't know much about relationships anyway.

And, like my parents, my husband was not emotionally available to me either. Essentially, I married a stranger. I had a stranger's babies. Even now, I talk about them as my children because he was not around to help raise them. My children were three years apart, and in between that time, while I was teaching school, I worked on a master's degree in counseling.

I was beginning to get a whiff of the shit, you know? A hint that something was wrong in myself and in our family. And I was gonna fix it. I thought I could control everything. So I continued in my workaholic behavior—doing mommyhood stuff, teaching school, and going to school. And missing the joy of just being myself and being with my family.

After I completed my master's degree, I got a job counseling students in a middle-school setting. I continued being very compulsive. I had no emotional boundaries. I didn't know where I stopped and the clients started.

For example, we had some kids at school who were living in their family car, and they were coming to school without their breakfast. I would come to school early and bring a little basket with eggs and fix the kids breakfast in the teachers' lounge. I thought it was my responsibility to take care of them when, in fact, probably half the other students didn't have breakfast either.

I also extended my work day. I stayed late to meet with parents. It was a real crazy time. I had a family, too, and a husband. But I didn't really want to know my husband then.

I worked at the school counseling job for about ten years. During that time, I completed yet another advanced degree as an educational specialist. After that, I thought I could manage a private practice because I already had the clientele. So I quit my job with the school and started a private practice working with children and families.

Around this time, my father-in-law's alcoholism was beginning to have an effect on my husband. Since I needed to control everything, I decided I would understand the alcoholism in the family. I thought I could fix my father-in-law and maybe my husband, too. Of course, I thought there was nothing wrong with me. I was functional.

I was also drinking alcohol. This was funny! I was going to understand alcoholism in these other family members. I had been using alcohol for twenty years by then. I began going to Al-Anon meetings because I heard you should do that if you were in a relationship with an alcoholic. I was in my late thirties at this time.

It was hard to catch that I was an alcoholic. I looked so good and only drank two drinks at most. I used to look around and compare myself to others who drank more than I did and think, "I couldn't be an alcoholic." It was at a training seminar that I began to catch on. A woman in the group said that an addiction was anything that you hide or that you lie about. I thought, "Oh, the game is up" because I knew I had been lying to myself about my alcohol use.

One of the ways I lied was by thinking that I never drank alone. I would go in my bedroom at home and drink my brandy while my husband was in the livingroom watching T.V., so I told myself I wasn't alone. Or I waited until my children went to bed, and I opened the liquor cabinet and fixed myself a drink—being very careful not to make any noise. Of course, later when I made my amends to them as part of my recovery in Alcoholics Anonymous, they told me they knew. They had heard everything.

I called my alcoholic husband from that training seminar and told him I thought I was an alcoholic. It was real hard for me to say that to him because he was my drinking buddy. There was dead silence on the other end of the line.

I didn't drink from then on. By then, I was forty-four years old. I began going to AA meetings and Workaholics Anonymous meetings in addition to Al-Anon meetings. I even became workaholic about all these twelve-step meetings, so now I just go to AA and Al-Anon.

As part of my recovery, instead of drinking or working hard, I began noticing what I was feeling. Becoming aware of what I was feeling and talking to others about it helped me to change. As I got further along in my recovery, it became clear that I could no longer work the way I had been.

I began to notice I couldn't stay focused with my clients anymore. I thought it was just a phase. But I continued to find my attention drifting out the window, you know, looking at the birds and the trees and wanting to be outside. Finally, I closed my private practice without knowing what I was going to do next. No work. That is a real test for a workaholic.

When I closed my private practice, I did continue leading a group on Saturdays. I also took a state government job working as a consultant to school counselors. I began to see how addictions work in organizations, particularly in government bureaucracy. People in bureaucracies are addicted to control. I was working with counselors to help students get in touch with their feelings. But school superintendents had trouble with that. I was told that children could not know what they felt until they were eighteen years old. Children were treated as objects in the school system.

I left that job after two years and took a part-time position working with women in prisons. I loved those women. I discovered our prisons are filled with nonrecovering addicts who are there on charges related to alcohol or drug addiction. I really cared for the women, but I couldn't stay very long. The prison system is deadly.

I took training in massage therapy and began to provide massage in addition to leading the Saturday group. By the time I left the prisons, I had a group and the massage clientele for financial support. So I just did that for awhile. I took some time to just pay attention to what was going on inside me and to what I needed.

I began to notice how much fun I was having doing massage. I loved being with people as they learned about themselves through touch. I located another massage therapist, and we opened the Massage Center about six months ago.

I work differently with people than I used to. When I was counseling, I believed I knew what clients should be feeling. I interpreted their feelings and thoughts for them. I used the counseling techniques I thought would help them reach where I thought they ought to be. If someone came in who had been sexually abused, I thought I knew just what they needed because, by God, I had been there myself! I would tell them what to do rather than listen to them as they talked about their feelings and experiences.

Now, I listen to my massage clients. Rather than working on someone, I try to work with them on what they need. The more I work this way, the more serene I become.

My own recovery included massage therapy. I had memories during massage that I didn't have access to before. Of course, we know now that memories are stored in the body. My addiction recovery has affected the way I work and the way I am.

A year after I joined AA, my husband recognized his own alcoholism and began his own recovery. Although we have been married for twenty-seven years, we now say that the first nineteen years we were not really in the relationship. Now we are finally getting to know each other.

It was difficult going through early recovery with my husband because so many issues came up—like control. For instance, he actually thought he owned me. We had to begin to talk about money and sex and trust. Trust was a big problem for me. I trusted no one.

We now have separate bank accounts and separate bedrooms, but we have a more intimate relationship. We share more of ourselves with each other on a deeper level. This has been a delightful outcome—one I didn't expect. We live our relationship day to day, and I still don't know if it will last. I know I would leave if I needed to in order to stay true to who I am.

Life is becoming more simple for me. I am becoming more quiet and more creative. As a child, I was such a hold-still, good little girl. Now I am enjoying movement, such as T'ai Chi and dance. I've been practicing T'ai Chi for about two years now, and I've integrated some of the movements into massage. I am more open to following something that might catch my interest. In the past I might have said, "You're almost fifty. You're too old to dance. Wouldn't you look ridiculous?"

When I opened the Massage Center, I said, "I'm almost fifty, and by God, I'm gonna do what I want to do. No more compromise." I welcome fifty. I would not trade this clarity I have for all the junk I carried around for the last thirty years.

Sixty Miles an Hour

Peg Curran

> My whole life, I've been doing things for other people.
> Now, if I don't want to eat, I don't have to eat. If I don't
> want to go home, I don't have to go home. Maybe that
> doesn't sound that important, but, when you've been
> somebody's daughter, and somebody's wife, and some-
> body's mother, and now you're just yourself, it's fabulous.

*"I'm doing what I want to do with my life, and I'm having a marvelous time. Age
doesn't mean a thing to me. Energy does, and, thank God, I have plenty of it."
Peg's throaty laughter and frequent gestures punctuate her conversation.*

*At sixty, Peg Curran has achieved her definition of success. She holds two
part-time jobs—one as a teacher in a French humanities program and another as a
sales representative/consultant for an art gallery. In her leisure time, she enjoys a
wide circle of friends who share her interests in art, writing, bridge, movies, and
world traveling.*

*Peg has crafted her present from a past that has often tested her strength and
flexibility. She is representative of a particular era of American women: women
who were raised to believe in the rightness of becoming a housewife in their teens or
early twenties, and who then—several years/children/homes later—encountered
what Betty Friedan, in the '60s, called "the feminine mystique."*

*Peg speaks poignantly about her experience with the feminine mystique. She
married a man she loved and admired not long after graduating from college. For
the next twenty years, she poured her energies into her family, her home, and
volunteer work. She also lost sight of her individuality.*

*Reading and reflecting about the women's movement were an important part of
Peg's awakening process. But it was when she accidentally discovered that she didn't
have to be afraid to speak publicly that she also discovered the courage to begin a
political career. She was forty years old. During the next twenty years, she has gradually tested herself in new arenas and learned more about her capabilities, her values,
and her feelings. She has also learned to act on and enjoy who she has become.*

*Peg refuses to acknowledge any roadblocks today. Clearly, she is a woman
who revels in her energy and in the adventures that life offers.*

Peg Curran

I grew up in Worcester, Mass. I'm a New Englander with all that comes with it. Strict father. Hilarious mother. She was good at telling jokes, and she drank her whiskey neat because she didn't like the taste of it.

I went to a high school for bright kids. I belonged to a debating society, everybody did. It was good for us. We debated lots of issues, and we never knew what side we would have to take. I graduated early because I skipped a few grades, so I was fifteen when I went away to college.

My mother was sure something terrible would happen to me, like I'd be sold into white slavery. I went to Columbia in New York. I had an uncle who lived in the Bronx, so I used to go out there to dinner on Sunday. And my uncle was sure, since I was going to Columbia, that I would become a communist. I used to do things like pick up a copy of *The Daily Worker* and take it with me to dinner just to annoy him.

I got a job at a magazine while I was still in school. I met my future husband, John, there. He was the ace reporter. We moved to John's hometown when his father got sick. It was a hard move. John told me all these things I was not to do. I was not to wear pants on the street. I was not to smoke on the street—I was a smoker in those days. I was especially not to smoke in front of his grandmother.

I was a good little housewife. I got rid of all my energy in good deeds. I served on lots of boards. I was on the library board, I was chair of the mental retardation board, the Y board, all that stuff. It was hard work, but it was hard work you didn't get paid for.

I always said, "If only I could talk, I'd be in politics." I had a terror of speaking, I really did. If I was secretary of something, I'd be so afraid I could hardly read the minutes.

One time, when I was president of a volunteer organization, I had to give a talk in public. I was terrified. Somebody taped the whole thing, and, when I heard myself later, I couldn't tell how terrified I was. That made me stop being afraid. It was like being afraid of being afraid, you know? If nobody could tell I was afraid, I was all right.

I thought maybe I would get into politics. I ran for city council. John was a big help. He did all of my advertising, he wrote the radio spots. I got elected, and it was a lot of fun. I found out I could do things. I never really knew I had a value before. I never knew it because I'd never gotten paid before for doing anything.

That probably was the beginning of my breaking out of being a housewife. I was forty. I'd been a good little girl up to then. I was old-fashioned and obedient. When John's car came up the driveway, I'd look out the window and think, "What did he tell me to do, and did I do it?"

In politics, I was the only woman on council, and I did a good job. That was sort of a surprise to me. It was also a surprise that I had respect from the men. My first night there—we had desks with blotters on them—somebody had replaced the green blotter that everybody else had with a pink one on my desk. I took the pink blotter off and threw it in the wastebasket. I did it without even thinking. [She laughs and grimaces.] But afterwards, I thought, maybe I'd hurt the feelings of whoever had put that pink blotter down, you know?

I was made chairman of the finance committee, which was a big thing. It turned out to be the power job on council. At that time, I was teaching three days a week—ninth grade at a private grade school—for free. I had time to work on council, and I worked hard. I didn't take anybody's word for anything, I would go out to look, to see what was happening. I found out things other people didn't know. I did my homework.

In spite of my husband's support, he never, ever came down to a council meeting. Not once in all the time I was on council. One night, I came home, and I'd had something really tough to do, I don't remember now what it was. And I came in, and he said, "Well, did you win?" And I said, "yes," and I burst into tears. And he said, "Don't cry," and I said, "Oh, what the hell good is my house? I'm down there, and I don't cry down there. If I can't cry at home, it's no good being here." And he said, "Cry, cry!"

I think crying is very beneficial. I used my car as my crying place. I'd get in the car and scream when I was driving down the road. Sometimes, probably, it wasn't very safe. I'd be crying so hard I couldn't see the road.

I decided maybe I would go to graduate school. I would never have had the courage to do that if I hadn't been reading about everything other women were doing. I had started reading everything I could on the women's movement, and that helped me.

I started a master's degree in liberal studies in a weekend program at a nearby university. I loved going back to school again after all those years. I could be a student forever.

It was hard on my marriage, though, because I guess John was threatened by it. I would come home all revved up and wanting to talk about philosophy or whatever—and he didn't want to hear it, didn't want to talk about it.

We argued. One time I said to him, "I will never walk three feet behind you again. I'll walk beside you, and, if you don't like it, that's too bad." I remember that argument—we were sitting on the front porch.

Anybody who's only been a housewife needs to know that she has value. You don't get that in a marriage. I know it's supposed to be fulfilling to be a wife and mother, but it isn't enough. If you're just at home with your husband and your children, you don't have anybody to debate with. I had a very good marriage as far as that goes, John was a bright guy. But I couldn't come home from school and talk about the things we talked about at school. To have somebody to argue with, to toss ideas back and forth with, that's good for you. It makes you feel good.

After I'd been on city council for two terms, I was talked into running for mayor, which was really a much bigger deal than I thought it was going to be. It turned out to be a dirty race. We had the windows shot out of our house. One Saturday morning, when I walked into the garage at 6:30 in the morning to get my car and drive to school, I saw that the car seats and tires had been slashed with a knife. That was terrifying.

My son was fifteen at the time, and I was warned that he might be set up to get into trouble. The rumors that got spread about our family were terrible. One time someone came up to me in public and said, "The story is that you lock your son in the closet." I laughed and said, "Oh, I wish!"

I lost the mayor's race by thirty votes. And that was a blow because I didn't know I would get that close. I knew I was running well because of the bad things that were happening to me. If they hadn't thought I had a chance, they wouldn't have gone after me.

When the next election came up, I got a lot of calls asking me to run again. The firemen called and said, "We have money to offer you, we didn't have money before." The downtown merchants called and said, "We need somebody intelligent." But I thought, "All my life I've been doing things for somebody else, now I'm through. I'm going to do what I want to do."

But then John got sick, and I took care of him until he died. I think it takes years after your husband dies before you become an individual again. We were married so long. We were even bound by our art collection. I had things hanging on the wall that I didn't like, but we had bought the art together. It was five years after he died, and they were still on the wall until, one day, I said to myself, "Take that down." It seemed disloyal, but that was nonsense.

I had a friend who ran a school-abroad program in France for American college students, a four-week intensive course. The year after John died, she asked if I would like to join them to teach art and humanities. I did, and I loved it.

The teaching was wonderful, but I felt alone over there. The one bright spot was one of the men who worked with us. He's much younger than I am.

We became lovers. It was good because I had somebody to talk to. It's good to have somebody who thinks you're special.

I had married somebody who was eleven years older than I was, and I didn't realize...I knew I had a lot of energy, a lot of sexual energy. I had always thought I was oversexed, but I'm not oversexed at all. And this lover in France let me know that I'm a perfectly normal person.

What was nice about the relationship was that everything was very easy and fun. There was no proving anything, no coming up to any standard. And so I went back again the next year.

I've been in the French program now for six years. The teaching is interesting. The students come from affluent families, but they have little cultural experience, and it's great to see them come alive. They've never set foot in a museum, they've never had to come up to standards. And being older, I have standards. If I set a deadline for a paper, for example, I don't care, they have to have the paper turned in that day.

It's exhausting work because you live with the students for the term, and you're essentially on twenty-four hours a day. They knock on my door at midnight sometimes about stuff that has nothing to do with school, like "So-and-so was mean to me," or, "Can I wear this blouse with this skirt?"

I'm not only their teacher, I guess I'm their mother, too. I find being with young people is good for me. It keeps me from being stodgy, it really keeps me on my toes. They write me letters later and tell me how much they enjoyed my classes and how much they enjoyed arguing with me in class. That's what I like to do—argue about ideas.

Two years ago, I started doing something else that's marvelous. I stopped in a gallery in town to see if they would be interested in buying any of the art John and I had collected over the years, and the man who owned the gallery came to see our collection. We went through the house, and he was overwhelmed by our stuff. We had bought it in the '60s for little money, but it's worth a lot now.

The gallery owner said, "You've really got an eye; how would you like to come work for me?" I thought I would try it out. It's been marvelous. Everything I ever wanted. Somebody said to me last night, "How lucky you are, you're doing everything you want." And I am. I'm doing exactly what I want. I'm not making much money, but that's okay. It doesn't take that much money to live. I've always had a lot of energy, but I always pushed it back. Now I have an outlet for it. I'm doing what I want without restrictions, too. John always kind of held me down. Now, if I want something, I go after it.

A friend of mine says women always feel they have to play what she calls "nice lady." And I'm not playing that anymore. I don't care if somebody doesn't like me. Maybe I say some things I shouldn't be saying, maybe I'm outrageous sometimes. I'm at the stage of life where I can say who the hell cares?

I like the gallery because I choose the artists we show. I do have a good eye for art. And the owner has confidence in my confidence. I work on commission, so I can come and go as I please. That's nice, it means I can travel when I want to. I enjoy the interaction with people in the gallery, talking to them about the art.

I'm doing something that's important. Art is a very important thing. Everybody has something that they love in life, and it's art with me.

And being single is good. I don't get lonely. I know there are people who can't stand being alone, but I'm not one of them. My whole life, I've been doing things for other people. Now, if I don't want to eat, I don't have to eat. If I don't want to go home, I don't have to go home.

Maybe that doesn't sound that important, but, when you've been somebody's daughter, and somebody's wife, and somebody's mother, and now you're just yourself, it's fabulous.

African Dancer

Adjawa Jones

Most of the dancers in my group are in their
forties....We're like a sisterhood. People who see us can't
believe we're all in our forties. It takes the audience by
surprise when our announcer tells them some of us are
even grandmothers. I think we inspire people to think
that age is not a barrier, that you can do whatever you
want to regardless of your age as long as you are in good
health.

*The throbbing sounds of the juju and cimba drums fill the auditorium; the audience
waits expectantly. The dancers come on stage, a whirling, pulsing cloud of gold
fabrics. Their movements are precise, yet sensual. The tempo of the music quick-
ens. The dancers' arms reach out, their knees lift high, every part of their bodies is
engaged in the dance—even their long black braids, which they toss for emphasis.
When the music reaches a climax, the audience roars its approval.*

*"You have to see me dance to know my story," Adjawa Jones, age forty-five,
told us. Adjawa (whose name means born on Monday) has a soft, gentle voice,
and, offstage, she is shy and reserved. She is a dark, slender woman whose easy,
graceful gestures mark her as a dancer who is at home in her body.*

*Adjawa's childhood was strongly influenced by a strict father who kept tight
control over his children's activities outside the family home. For Adjawa, African
dancing symbolizes the freedom of movement she did not have growing up. Over
the years, the dancing has also become a way to teach African-Americans and
others about African traditions.*

*What entering midlife has brought to Adjawa is a clear and exciting identifica-
tion with her African roots. Her mature pride in who she is has allowed her to become
comfortable putting her hair in braids and wearing African clothing to work.*

*She has also re-arranged her priorities in life. With her husband's full support,
she no longer worries about keeping an immaculate home and cooking regular
dinners. Instead, Adjawa is focused on the dancing, which she sees as a vehicle for
connecting with people as well as an opportunity for expressing herself*

Adjawa Jones

I was born and raised in Rochester, the second youngest of five kids. My father was very, very strict. We had a curfew and weren't allowed out after nine o'clock. Even my eighteen-year-old brothers—they had to be on the porch or in the house by 9 p.m.

We didn't live in a great part of town, so that's why we had to be in our house at a certain time. My father didn't let us venture off too far. He felt that, if he didn't know the other families, then he didn't know what would happen to us. We didn't do a lot of things the other kids did. We weren't even allowed to go to football games.

We kept the family whole. We all had to take care of each other and look after each other. My mother was a very giving person. She was like a saint. We all went to the Baptist church every Sunday except for my father who stayed home. It was an all-day thing. We wouldn't get out till two o'clock, and sometimes we'd go back in the evening for evening services.

I went to a neighborhood school, an average school. We learned a lot, had fun. My father would wait for us after school across the street. Sometimes, when I knew he was there, I would bug out the back. I would just kind of do what I wanted to do. Sometimes, I would get into trouble. My sister would take the blame, or I would get a spanking. Most of the time, though, we toed the line.

There was always the respect—"Yes, ma'am," or "yes, sir." And we were told to use the same respect when we went to our friends' houses. If we did do something we shouldn't have, their mothers would call and say, "We saw your daughter doing such and such, and I told her..." That was the mothers' network. I have a lot of good memories of high school even though my father didn't let us get involved in a lot of activities. We were allowed to go to church and be involved in youth groups. I did have a date to go to the prom, but my older brother came along.

I can look back now and laugh at all the things my father didn't let us do. It's a big joke now. I said I would never be as strict with my kids, but I am similar. I find myself saying to them, "I need to know who you're going with and where you're going." My husband was brought up in the same way, so we have similar philosophies on raising our kids.

I went to community college for a while after high school, then to the university. I thought about majoring in business. When I was twenty-two, I got married to my high school sweetheart—the one I went to the prom with.

I continued to take classes in the day, and I would normally be home in the evening trying to be the so-called "good wife," like always having dinner on the table. I didn't do too many other things. I just stayed home and did hobbies, like crocheting.

I had my son, and, when he was ready for school, we wanted him to find his cultural roots. We found a good African preschool for him. He really enjoyed it. That was when my husband and I began getting into our culture, too.

All the parents from the African school would meet once a week to plan various functions. We would talk about our kids and how we wanted to keep the school going because it was always just barely making it. Once a month, we'd have a social event and everybody would bring an ethnic dish. We had fundraisers, and parents would help cook food or sell tickets. They had little graduation ceremonies for the kids, and the parents would help make African costumes for the kids to wear.

When I had my daughter, we got her in the school, too. We were trying to get the kids to find their roots and find their place. They got the nurturing they needed in the African school, and they really did well.

By the time my daughter was two, I started getting into African dance. It started out just as exercise, and it gave me peace of mind. At first, I was doing it to get a little time away from the kids, but then they started coming with me when my husband had to work late.

Several of us women decided to form a dance group. We saw it as a way of staying within the African culture, of learning about our roots, and then of trying to educate other people as we performed. We asked our families to join in the group. My daughter is still dancing with us. My husband and my son were involved when it first started, but they've grown away from it now.

Over the years, as we learned more about our culture, the dance group has gradually expanded its activities. For example, we celebrate rites of passage. When my daughter turned thirteen, starting into womanhood, we had a rite. Adults have passages, too, like maybe from the ages of forty to forty-five or forty-five to fifty.

We help to build roadways for young people to follow. We call this nation building, helping other members in the community, giving them role models to follow or helping them in any way we can.

Sometimes we go to schools and give lecture demonstrations about culture and dance from different parts of Africa. We let even the first graders have a chance on the drums and other instruments. We also teach the dances to kids from the neighborhoods. Sometimes I teach beginning dancing to children from four to six years old.

I have learned from master dancers who have been to Africa and brought the dances back. We believe in passing things down. When a master teaches us something, we share it with our daughters and everyone in the community who wants to learn it. We look at our dancing as a spiritual connection between people.

I've worked as a secretary in a research center for three years now. I've worked most of the time I've been married and had the kids. When they were little, I went to school to be a dental assistant. I was an honor student, which was exciting for me then—realizing I could go to school and be a mother. I worked as a dental assistant for a little while, but then I became a secretary. Pay-wise, it's about the same.

When I turned forty, I decided to make my statement: I started putting my hair into corn-row braids. I never wore braids before, I'd just wear my hair long or put it up in a bun or whatever. My statement meant that I had come into myself as an over-forty woman and that I had come into my pride in my African-American heritage. I don't think you have to turn forty to be proud of being an African-American, but I didn't start coming into my pride until then.

It did take a while to feel comfortable with the braids. I thought everybody was looking at me. After I accepted the braids, I said, "Well, I don't care what everybody else thinks. This is me." Then it no longer bothered me.

I also decided to start wearing African clothing to work sometimes—the everyday business dress styles without the head wraps. I wouldn't have thought of it before. It makes me feel special when I wear this clothing. The colors are so lively that they brighten my face up and make me feel energetic.

What has also changed since I've turned forty is that I'm no longer the nice home-baby I used to be. Now, I'm hardly home. And I don't have dinners ready like I used to. I'm out in the community all the time. Like last night, we danced at a fundraiser for a political party. This afternoon, we are dancing at a wedding. It was a last-minute invitation, so I won't have time to clean my house or get home to make dinner. I probably won't be home until eight or nine. But I'm not tired because the dancing energizes me. I'm in my culture.

My husband doesn't mind although my change has meant a change for him, too, at home. But he's always been very supportive. He doesn't mind me staying out late because he knows I'm doing my thing and I'm happy. And he notices a growth in me. I think I get a lot of pleasure from the dancing because I was so cooped up as a child, held back so strictly.

Most of the dancers in my group are in their forties. The one who started the group is fifty-one, and she's been dancing for years. We come from all different backgrounds, but we connect. We're like a sisterhood. People who see us can't believe we're all in our forties. It takes the audience by surprise when our announcer tells them some of us are even grandmothers. I think we inspire people to think that age is not a barrier, that you can do whatever you want to regardless of your age as long as you are in good health.

The dancing is good exercise. As I get older, it helps me to keep my weight down. And I enjoy African dancing because it's a way for me to express myself. I don't normally communicate well by talking. If I had to talk in front of people, I'd be nervous. But I can do it through dance and song.

The dancing keeps me mentally young, too. Sometimes, I've told myself, "I'm getting older, and I shouldn't be dancing anymore." But if I haven't been dancing for a week or two, my body starts stiffening up, my legs start hurting. It's hard to get out of bed. When I'm dancing, I don't feel any of these aches and pains.

My nephew asked me the other day how long I was going to dance. I think I'm going to do it just as long as I can. Our leader is fifty-one, and she isn't planning on retiring. One of our master dancers is in his sixties, but he doesn't look sixty at all.

Maybe I know I can't do some of the moves like I used to. My knees aren't coming up as high as they used to. But I can still hang in there with the best. After a performance, my adrenaline is flowing. It's a natural high. You don't come down for two hours. You stay pumped up, and you feel good about yourself. You feel good that you're sharing your culture. You feel good when you give your all to something.

A Girl from Queens

Judith Katz

> My mother's death made me realize how short life is. It
> made me question what was most important. I wondered
> how much I needed to accomplish to make a difference
> that really mattered....I think getting married was about
> taking care of me. I finally realized I didn't have to lose
> who I was in the world to be able to have love and sup-
> port in my life.

*Many women's stories begin with the experiences of their parents and even grand-
parents. Traumatic events of previous generations may haunt and profoundly influence the course of some women's lives. They may not even be aware of how this
legacy has shaped their values until later in life as they go through a period of
assessment.*

*Judith Katz (her real name), a forty-two-year-old organizational consultant
and author, is the daughter of Jewish Holocaust survivors. She has always been
responsive to issues of injustice and oppression. Throughout her career as an edu-
cator and consultant, she has addressed empowerment, racism, and sexism.*

*As Judith approached forty, she found herself longing for a personal life. Suc-
cess in her career was no longer enough. Her mother's illness and death when
Judith was thirty-nine led to a period of self-examination, culminating in new
decisions and directions based on her own needs for care and support. And she
began to allow herself to be more tender and vulnerable. At age forty, Judith married a man she had fallen in love with the year before.*

*At forty-two, Judith is a woman of considerable energy—"on warp speed,"
her friends say. But she is beginning to notice some limitations on how much she
can do and struggles with how much she wants to continue to push herself.*

*And, like most of us, she is facing other physical changes as well. The clothes
on her size four frame don't fit quite the same as they used to. Her dark, curly hair
is sprinkled with gray. A breast biopsy and the signs of menopause are now part of
her experience. She talks openly about these changes and encourages all of us to do
the same.*

Judith Katz

Both my parents are German Jews. My father left when he was seventeen. There was a warrant for his arrest during *Kristallnacht*. Many Jews were being rounded up and taken to the camps then, and my father and my grandfather decided it was time to leave (my grandmother got out later).

My father had a three-year-old cousin who they were going to take with them. But when they got to the Dutch border, they found they didn't have the right papers for this little boy. They had to go back to Dusseldorf and leave the boy there with his parents. My father and my grandfather hid for a week and then finally got out. But the little boy and his parents, my father's aunt and uncle, could not escape and later died in a concentration camp. My father felt both very grateful for surviving and very much ashamed that he couldn't do something to protect this little boy. This was a very big issue in his life.

I was named after this aunt and uncle who were killed in the camp. Talk about a legacy of what you are in the world to do. As I have looked back at my life, I see that I was deeply influenced —although unconsciously—by my family's experience of oppression.

My mother and her family left Germany in 1933 when she was nine. Her father was told by a neighbor who had just joined the Gestapo, "You better get out of Germany. It looks bad for the Jews." My mother never remembered anything about her experiences in Germany. She didn't want to remember.

My mother was tough. Her nickname was "the fucking wonder." She could do almost anything—very smart and very talented. She grew up in the streets of New York. She was outspoken and direct and often used four-letter words. I really thought this was normal. I thought this was how you talked. My father would say to me, "That's no way for a lady to talk." I would respond, "It doesn't matter. I don't want to be a lady, you know? I want to be like my mother. She's tough. She's all right." That was my role model for how a strong woman could be.

When I was about sixteen, my mother went to school for pattern making and dress designing. She was offered a job as an assistant designer in New York. She didn't take the job because she said, "It's a choice between your father or this career." I believed that. I now believe that was only part of her truth. At the time, I didn't see her fear or lack of self-confidence.

So I grew up thinking, if it's a choice between a relationship and a career, I'm taking a career. I also recall being told by my parents that, if I was going to college, it was going to be Queens College—which was right down the street—or no college. Because the money was needed for my younger brother in the event he wanted to go away to school.

I always believed I wasn't very smart. I was an average student. My friends made it into an accelerated program, but I didn't. I didn't do well on standardized tests. I always had to work hard for my grades. We didn't have many books in the house, and my parents didn't read to me. But my parents did value education as something good to have.

I remember the first time I had an article published after completing my doctorate. I called my grandmother, feeling excited and proud of my accomplishment. Her response was, "How much did they pay you?" If they don't pay you, it can't mean anything, you know? My family came out of the merchant class and often measured accomplishment in terms of how much you are making rather than the nature of the work.

As an adolescent, I didn't see myself as attractive. I wore braces and often felt tormented by peers who called me "Brillo" and "grapefruit pits" because of my curly hair and flat chest. I used to ask boys out, so I didn't have to go through the anxiety of waiting to see if anybody asked me.

At one time, I had a dream of being one of the first computer scientists. I became a math major in college and completed most of the math requirements. Then I had this professor—I'll never forget—it was clear he did not like women. The women were weeded out. You could see. At first, there were six of us, then there were four of us, then two of us. I got a D in this course and said, "That's it. I'm out of here." I transferred to elementary education. Math wasn't as much fun as dealing with people anyhow, and I had probably been hanging on longer than I should have.

In college, I became active in civil rights activities—both on and off campus—and in human relations training. These activities were vital to me. I went to a workshop in my senior year where eighty-five percent of the participants were people of color. By the end of the week, it was clear to me that racism was a critical issue to address. I began to identify how I as a white woman could effect change in the white community. It wasn't about changing blacks or helping blacks. That's really where my career started to take shape. I knew this was what I had to do as my work.

I think I went straight through graduate school because of what my mother had said about career and marriage, and, believing the choice to be between them, I chose a career.

I still didn't have a lot of confidence, though. I was very insecure, and I still am in a lot of ways. My self-concept was of not being good enough, and my achieving was always to prove that I was okay. When I did my dissertation, I had to rewrite and rewrite. My language skills were really poor. I might get the ideas conceptually, but my grammar stunk. I had an English professor in college who gave me a C and told me, "You don't know how to read, and you don't know how to write." I believed it, and I guess I saw it as unchangeable for many years.

I remember once while writing my dissertation, I was on the bathroom floor in a fetal position crying, saying, "I'll never finish this. I can't do this. I'm not capable." I called my parents. My father, trying to be supportive, said, "You don't have to finish it if you don't want to. We'll still love you." I really wanted him to say, "You can do it. Stop being a jerk here!" The part of my mother I had in me thought, "Fuck it. I'm gonna do this!" I completed my dissertation, which was an anti-racism training program for whites. It was published as a book in 1978 and is still being used in training.

When I completed my doctorate, I was twenty-five. I accepted a job offer from the University of Oklahoma, teaching in a master's program focused on human relations training, organizational development, and issues of racism and sexism.

It was very hard for me to live in Oklahoma, especially as a feminist and as someone working on the problems of racism. I had to learn how to deal with people and issues differently. It wasn't like the Northeast where you could assume people didn't want to be racist or sexist. In Oklahoma, many people were more overt about their racist and sexist attitudes.

In many ways, I was rather naive. I had lived there two weeks when I was raped. Someone broke into my apartment. Talk about things your parents say to you! My mother always said, "Get an apartment on the second floor. Don't leave your windows open." I thought, "This isn't New York. I don't have to worry about these things."

As a feminist, I knew that the rape was not my fault. Rape is an issue of violence. Knowing that helped tremendously. But the experience was very painful and frightening. There were many nights that I didn't sleep. I often say, "I'm fine. I'm fine," when I'm not fine. About six months later, a friend said to me, "I know you're doing fine, but there still may be stuff you want to talk about."

It's like when somebody dies. Initially, everybody is around, then everybody leaves. And it gets to a point where it's not okay to talk about it. People think it should be done with. They think, "Yeah, that happened a couple of months ago and it was terrible, but life goes on."

My friend came over on a Saturday with a bottle of wine. We spent hours and hours talking and crying. I knew in my head that I wasn't to blame. But emotionally, I was feeling that I shouldn't have kept my window open. I shouldn't have done this or shouldn't have done that. I wondered if there was some way I could have avoided it. I learned that, no matter how much you know intellectually, the emotional level is different.

Several months later, I started talking publicly about the rape—in forums and classes. It's not like it took a lot of courage. It was my way to heal and to make sense of what had happened. When I started talking about being raped, I found out how many women in my life had been raped. How pervasive it is—abuse, rape, incest. It's the silent part of our lives.

My years at the University of Oklahoma were very challenging. I used to speak about it much more negatively. I learned a lot about politics as I successfully went through the tenure process. I think as women we believe, "If I just do my job, my work will speak for itself." But that's not the game.

I was thirty-three when I started having a recurring dream about being a shriveled-up prune. I wanted to leave Oklahoma, but I was terrified. The dream seemed to be telling me that, if I stayed much longer, I would shrivel up and die.

I attended a meeting in San Diego and fell in love with that city. There was no question about it, this was where my soul was! I decided to take a leave of absence from my university position and moved to San Diego two years later without a job. I just decided this was where I wanted to be. I thought, "It'll work out."

Several months later, I accepted a job at San Diego State University. At the same time, I began a partnership with an organizational consultant whose business partner had recently died. That has evolved into the work I'm still doing. We support corporations in using cultural diversity within their organizations to make their business stronger. What is wonderful is that it isn't work to me. It's my life—dealing with racism and sexism in and out of the workplace.

I only taught at San Diego State for a year. I was done with higher education. But during that year, on the days I didn't teach, I would take the red-eye flight to work with my consulting clients. I was having a great time.

The consulting work was very challenging and seductive. I felt powerful and valued. I flew first class on the Concorde to places like Singapore. I was working with major corporations and making an impact in addressing issues of racism and sexism, so it was easy to put a lot of my energy there.

I started to make a lot of money. A lot of money. I was extremely successful. But, I thought, "So what?" My schedule was grueling. I was sometimes gone a month at a time. And when I came home, I had to deal with being alone. The issue of not having a personal life was getting bigger and bigger. Finally, I told my business partner we would have to make some changes. I had to have a life. I had to find some balance.

I started going to therapy in a serious way. In the past, I would go to therapy long enough to deal with the crisis and then be gone. And it always looked like I was fine. People would always think I was handling things great.

I was discovering in therapy that the work was a way for me to run away from the personal side of my life. (A therapist once asked me how I could be so good professionally and so screwed up personally.) I often felt in control and competent in my professional world, but fearful that, if people really knew who I was personally, they wouldn't care about me.

I also decided about this time that I was going to be single the rest of my life. This was a paradox! I wanted to have a life, but I wanted to put it on hold. My mother taught me that, if you got married, you had to give up who you were. I also didn't think I could find a man who would want me or who could support me emotionally—or in my professional life. In the past, I never felt I was being taken care of by a man. Or that, if I was really raggedy, they would be there for me. It was important to me to face being single. I wanted to be happy in my life as it was.

I decided to remodel my house. I wanted to make it into my dream home. I believe our house is often a metaphor for our lives. Remodeling this house was about creating my life the way I wanted, about being able to work and to visualize what I wanted in this house—I still get chills about it. It was the most beautiful house. I still cry over leaving it.

At the same time, I was getting a little more balance in my life and having a little more fun. I started having more of a social life, developing a network of friends unrelated to work. I needed to face some issues in myself about being Jewish. It was time to stop avoiding it. I decided to start seeing some Jewish men.

That year I received a card from David, a man I knew when I was in college. We kept bumping into each other over the years, but I was not particularly attracted to him. After one of these meetings, he wrote me a note saying, "I wonder why I still think about you after sixteen years?"

I carried this note around for weeks in my briefcase because this was the third time he had popped up in my life. I believe people come back into our lives for a reason. I thought seeing him might be part of clearing out my past, so I could move on to the future.

He lived in Washington, D.C. I planned to be there on business, so I went to dinner with him. He turned out to be very loving and very caring. I had had a lot of relationships where sex was the connecting point. This was not that. So this was all the more confusing for me. For both of us. But being with him was wonderful—the conversations, how I was treated. I felt taken care of and valued. This was different. After the third or fourth time I saw him, he told me he loved me. I was scared.

The year I turned thirty-nine, a lot happened. My mother died in January. I spent a week with her several months before she died. It was a wonderful week of deep connection, of sharing and tears and saying goodbye. I learned a lot about when strength is weakness and weakness is strength. It was hard for her to ask for help—to be vulnerable. I saw so much of myself in her. What I had defined as my strength was not my strength.

I think understanding this was partly what enabled me to get married. Because so much of my pushing away is what I saw my mother do—what everybody said was her strength. She could express her anger; she couldn't express her hurt.

Soon after she died, my house was finished. By now most of my work was on the East Coast. I was commuting every week and fitting in time with David in Washington. Even though I had this wonderful house that was just completed, it was clear that I wasn't going to live there. I kept it for about five months and then sold it. David and I bought a home together in D.C.

My mother's death made me realize how short life is. It made me question what was most important. I wondered how much I needed to accomplish to make a difference that really mattered. I also realized I needed to take better care of myself. Talk about change. I think getting married was about taking care of me. I finally realized I didn't have to lose who I was in the world to be able to have love and support in my life. And he was special in that he came fully wrapped. He came with his career—his life. He didn't need to get married. I didn't need to get married. Getting married was my fortieth birthday present to myself and David's gift to me.

Our wedding was a wonderful celebration. We were married by a dear friend rooted in Jewish philosophy and culture who merged those traditions with other traditions important to us. The ceremony represented who we were as a couple—our values and our lives. For both of us, justice and valuing diversity are important elements of our lives. We invited two hundred people. The room was full of wonderfully diverse people—people we had known for twenty-thirty years.

After we were married, people asked me, "Are you going to work?" Why would I not work? This has been my life. I didn't get married to stop my life. I got married to add to my life.

The past few years have been emotionally tough, though, like internal white-water rafting. I spent a week in bed crying about my mother not being there. As I was going through it, another part of me, like a third eye, was saying, "You need to go through this. This is important." Knowing I needed to do this was the calm part. Even though I felt miserable, just going through this pain gave me inner confidence.

Allowing myself to be vulnerable doesn't terrify me now as much as it used to. Now I get terrified for an hour instead of for two days. I know I need to do this to move myself along this path—whatever this path is.

I miss my mother a lot. I have a lot of questions to ask her. Being forty-two, I want to know what she went through with menopause. As women, I think we still don't share enough about the aging process —how our lives change. Nobody talks about menopause. So much of sexism is based on our being young and attractive. What about as we get older?

I am aware that my body is changing. I had a breast biopsy last year, which turned out to be nonmalignant. But we talk about a biopsy like it is nothing. We don't talk about how frightening it is to go through that and wait for the test results. We don't want to talk about our bodies. We don't want to talk about those changes.

I've started having hot flashes. I never felt that way before. I thought I could be crazy. No one really prepares you for it. It's one of the silent subjects.

Recently, I developed an allergy and couldn't wear makeup for months. I've always worn makeup, but I've stopped wearing it altogether now. This is a major change. Wearing makeup is what I grew up with as a woman. So now—this is my face and this is who I am.

I wonder why we just can't accept who we are? I have not dyed my hair. People started saying, "Oh, you've got a lot of gray in your hair." Well, what's wrong with having gray in my hair? When women get older, they lose their attractiveness, which means they lose their power. As men get older, they become more powerful and more attractive. These are the myths of sexism.

I feel like I'm completing a set of transitions—from seeing myself as a little girl from Queens to really experiencing myself as a powerful woman. At times, I have a vision of winning a Nobel Peace Prize. I don't know how I would do that, but it's a symbol for me of influencing people, policies, and structures in an ever larger way. I don't know about the Nobel Peace Prize. I do know I'm committed to creating change.

I can see that life is too short—no matter how long it is. On this side of forty, I recognize that I want to live my life fully. I'm feeling a little more freedom now to do that. I worry less about how other people are going to see me or feel about me. I don't take myself as seriously, and yet I take who I am dead seriously.

As I get older and my energy changes, it's easier to stay comfortable—to stay stuck. I know people think I'm on warp speed, but I don't feel that way internally. I rest more these days. But I am grateful to the people in my life who have known that it's important for me not to stay stuck and will fight with me about it.

It is important to my identity to continue to challenge myself. When I was teaching at the university, I saw colleagues whose notes got yellower and yellower each year. The pages would start crumbling. I knew that was not how my life would be.

Dream Weaver

Sylvia Michaels

> Essentially, I see things differently now. I have a great
> sense of urgency to do some of the projects I thought I'd
> always have time to do. It's a year later now, and I'm
> glad I've had another year....I'm going to have that hope
> for another five years. Then I will think I'm technically
> cured—although, having gone through something like
> this, you never have that same sense of security again.

At the time of this writing, breast cancer in women is epidemic. Being over forty, and especially over fifty, puts women at greater risk. But as frightening as the diagnosis of breast cancer is, it doesn't mean that dreams can't be realized. The diagnosis may even prompt a period of reflection and generate a new sense of purpose in life.

Sylvia Michaels is a forty-three-year-old woman whose story sheds a light on the problems women face with mastectomies and breast implants. In spite of the harsh physical realities involved in the treatment and recovery process, Sylvia insists on moving forward with her life.

Sylvia has earned a good living as a professional sales person representing products and services to health care providers. When she was diagnosed with breast cancer a year ago, she was determined to treat the cancer as an "inconvenience" and maintain a positive attitude. But the day came that she had to stop denying the seriousness of the mastectomy and face it for the loss that it was. The healthy anger she experienced as part of the grieving process helped her focus her energy on creating new opportunities and fulfilling long-held, personal dreams.

Sylvia is a petite ash blond with large blue eyes. She speaks in a low, well modulated voice—a professional-sounding voice that has made many successful sales presentations. She tells her story sitting on a couch in her livingroom. Behind her is a library table with pictures of family and friends from all over the world. This is her favorite place to sit and relax. From here, she can see the faces of the many people who are important in her life.

Sylvia Michaels

I was born in a small rural area in Pennsylvania up near the New York state border. My mother was a nurse. She was in her late twenties by the time she saved up enough money to be able to get her training.

My dad also went to school later in life—he put himself through school. I understood from the sacrifices they made that education was something to be valued. There was never a question in my mind that I wouldn't go away to school, that I wouldn't have a career, that I wouldn't be able to do with my life whatever I wanted.

I got married when I was a college sophomore. I was a pre-law student until after my daughter was born, and then I switched to sociology. I felt that I wouldn't be able to go directly from undergraduate school to law school when I had a small child.

After I graduated, I was shocked to be asked questions during job interviews that I thought were absolutely absurd and had no bearing on my ability to do the job. Things like, "What kind of birth control do you use? If your child is ill, how are you going to make sure that you don't have to stay home to take care of it? What's going to happen if you and your husband get a promotion at the same time?"

It irritated me that companies had the right to pry into my personal life. I had made the decision that I was always going to have a career, and I would provide for myself and my family. I found the interview questions to be really archaic. I didn't think people could ask things like that, and now, thank God, they can't legally.

I realized after I had been married for several years that my husband didn't have the same ambition that I did. I had always looked at him as being smarter than I was. I'm not sure where that came from because I never saw my mother apologize to or back down from any man. I never knew why I thought my husband would be this white knight in shining armor because that wasn't the way I was raised. For some reason, I thought that I would always work, I'd have my own career, but he would be the one who made the most money, who was the most important. I'd make all the sacrifices, moving and supporting his career.

And all of a sudden, I realized that he was never going to be that white knight. I thought if I was not going to be happy living the kind of life he would provide, I better make a decision and make things happen for myself. I went ahead and decided I was going to get the first promotion, I was going to move up the corporate ladder, and I was going to be someone who could take care of herself financially and emotionally and everything else, and, if he wanted to come along for the ride, that would be fine. If he couldn't, well, then that would be fine.

I think I had already made up my mind that the marriage was basically over. But with my background of Catholicism and the commitment to keep the family together because we had a child, I didn't go through with a divorce.

I was offered a promotion and transferred to Connecticut. I lived by myself in an apartment in Connecticut for a year and commuted back and forth to Pennsylvania to see my family. My daughter stayed with her father. He finally decided he would come and join me there, and then I got a fantastic job offer in Arizona and uprooted everybody again. That had a price because we eventually did get a divorce.

After I lived in Arizona for a while, I went back to school and completed an MBA, which was, to me, a major accomplishment. Except for working in sales, I had no business background, so I had to work very hard for that degree.

When I met Greg, I was pretty happy with who I was and comfortable with where I was going. He was the first man I ever met who is comfortable with the soft side of himself. He is very caring and very supportive. I was thirty-six when we got married.

I thought we might have a child together because more older women are having children these days. But then in blending two families—he has two children—and his daughter moved in with us, and my daughter was a year younger than his—we thought we owed these existing children more than bringing another child into the world.

When I was forty-two, I went to my gynecologist for a pap test and said, "I think it's time for another mammogram." We have no history of breast cancer in the family, so I didn't think I was at risk. I was just doing it because the medical guidelines say you should have a mammogram every two years after you turn forty.

I had the mammogram at one o'clock and, about a quarter to five when I got home, there was a message on the machine. It was the breast center, and they said there's something abnormal, and they wanted me to come back in.

I thought it was just an inconvenience, but I went in and had a full series of tests. Greg was in Europe. I was not tremendously concerned, and they didn't seem to be terribly concerned. The radiologist and the nurse wanted to do an ultra-sound; they said it was probably just a cyst.

Then I had to wait for the surgeon to do a biopsy. He sent the specimen down to the lab, and it came back, and I thought it was okay, and I thought, "Thank you, God." Then the surgeon said, "I don't think we biopsied the right place. We have to do it again." By that time, it was 5:30. He said, "Don't wait. Go home."

By the time I got home, I was pretty crazed. But I had already made up my mind, if I had to have a mastectomy, screw it. I wanted to go forward. I had kind of a bad time that night waiting. My daughter Holly came up to spend the next day with me. The doctor called about three o'clock and said, yes, it was cancer. At first, I was very philosophical and wanted to look ahead. But that weekend, I had a hysterical, this-can't-be-happening-to-me kind of experience.

I thought it couldn't happen to me because I came from a family with good genes. My grandparents—all four of them—lived a long time. My parents have always taken good care of themselves. I had a false sense of security.

Then, right away, I got wrapped up in the decision-making process. I had to meet the plastic surgeon, the radiologist, the oncologist, and each one of them told me what my options were. My surgeon was pushing for a lumpectomy, and I said, "I just can't live with that. If the one breast is gone, then all I have to worry about is the other one. I don't want to deal with the lumpectomy." I went for a second opinion because I wanted to make sure that they were right and that, if there was some other procedure available, I would have that option.

A wonderful woman I know runs a breast center in Northern California. I called her right away, and she became my sounding board. I'd call her throughout all of this and say, "I saw the doctor, and he told me such and such. What does it mean?" And she'd say, "You don't need to worry about it," or "You need to go back and ask him this."

My friend Sandra, who is a nurse, and my husband went with me to all the interviews with doctors. Sandra knew the medical jargon. She could catch things I might miss, and Greg could ask things from a layperson's point of view. My daughter went with us, too, so I had this wonderful security net of people to go through it with me.

I had decided I wanted a breast implant. After the mastectomy, they put in an expander. They expand it by putting in saline over a period of two months. They keep stretching the skin so that it will accommodate the implant. Then they overextend it, so the skin will droop somewhat to look like the other breast.

I had the implant surgery in mid-March. The expander was removed, and they put the implant in. Then they wait a couple of months to do the reconstruction of the nipple.

Several years before all this happened, I had started a running regimen, and I was running three or four miles a day. I was eager to get back on the program as soon as I could after the first expander surgery. I asked the plastic surgeon when I could start exercising again. He told me I could probably start walking three or four days after the surgery. I did, and I started back on my Nordic Track. I didn't use my arms, just my legs. About five days later, I became terribly uncomfortable with the expander.

My plastic surgeon was out of town, so I went to see another surgeon. I was afraid I had moved the expander. The surgeon looked at it and said it looked fine. I wasn't satisfied with that, so I left a message for my plastic surgeon to call me when he got back. He called and asked what was wrong. When I told him about the Nordic Track, he went crazy, just crazy.

He said, "Don't you realize we might have to do another surgery?" I told him I wasn't using my arms, so what the hell did my legs have to do with it? He said, "Oh, well, you're probably okay." After I got off the phone, I started crying. I called him back, and said, "I'm trying to be a good patient, I didn't mean to make you angry. Don't yell at me." The next day, when I went in to see him, he said, "I didn't yell at you." It was just the strangest exchange.

I kept up a regimen of exercise and eating healthy and doing all this shit all through the chemotherapy and everything, thinking, when this is all over, I'm going to feel fine. And then I started to have to deal with menopause because the chemotherapy threw me into menopause. It was like— screw this! And now I can't take hormone replacement, so I have to have hot flashes. I didn't bargain for all this, but I don't think it would have changed my decision. I probably would have still had to have chemotherapy even if I had the lumpectomy.

Chemotherapy was the hardest thing I've ever had to deal with. I'd feel fine for the first twenty-four hours, the second day I noticed that nothing tasted good, and everything smelled horribly. The smell of food, the thought of food—and then the third day, for the first six treatments, I felt okay, but not quite right. By the fourth day, I felt fine.

The seventh treatment was right after Thanksgiving, and Greg was gone. I thought it would be the same as the others. But by the next day, I was so sick I thought I was going to die. The eighth one was just before Christmas, and I had started teaching my first marketing class. Teaching had always been one of my goals, and I thought I'd better take care of these goals now because I don't have time to put them off anymore. Psychologically, it took everything I had to go on working and teaching. I kept thinking, "This is just not happening."

By the end of January, I was finished with the chemotherapy, and I thought then, "I just have to get through these other two implant surgeries, and then I'll be home free." Then I had the menopause on top of that.

But no one said to me—and I talked with a lot of women—that it's never going to be okay, that you're not going to feel the same way physically that you did before. I never heard anyone complain about discomfort, but the implant wasn't comfortable to me. I kept feeling like I needed to move it all the time.

I think the women I talked with didn't warn me partly because they wanted to put the experience behind them. As far as they were concerned, the worst part of it was over when they had the surgery. They weren't going to dwell on the fact that it wasn't going to be perfect. I kept thinking, "There must be something wrong with me because this is not okay. This does not feel good."

When I have been more tired or under more stress, I've felt real uncomfortable, and I've just wanted to rip the damn thing out of my chest. And then there have been other days when it's perfectly fine. I think the implant's beginning to feel a little more normal.

I had wanted to think of the mastectomy as just an inconvenience, I didn't want it to slow me down. But your body can't go through all of that turmoil and assault and just be fine. I'm sure that my positive attitude was a plus for me. There also came the point when I had to face reality, and the reality is that a mastectomy is a maiming of your body.

It's real aggravating. There's so little that's known about the cause of breast cancer or how to prevent it. There's so little attention given to women's health issues—including menopause. That's making me very angry. Especially now when I know my daughter will be at risk.

Essentially, I see things differently now. I have a great sense of urgency to do some of the projects I thought I'd always have time to do. It's a year later now, and I'm glad I've had another year. I'm hoping I have another year. I'm going to have that hope for another five years. Then I will think I'm technically cured—although, having gone through something like this, you never have that same sense of security again. Because now every little thing that feels different in my body, I wonder what it is.

Right now, I'm putting my energy into a new business venture. Last year around Christmas, I got an idea for making fabric Christmas wrapping. I talked the idea over with a friend, who is a seamstress and an engineer, and we began planning. We've spent our spare time in the past year shopping and playing with fabrics —looking for fabric with the right kind of stretch and look. Now we have a prototype done. We have demonstration pieces ready, manufacturing capabilities set up, the fabric identified. Our plan is in place. By the end of the month, we'll be ready to take orders.

I used to sew, and I have done many arts and crafts in the past. I used to do macrame and tinsel painting. But for years, I haven't done anything creative. I always thought I would get back to it someday, so this feels good.

Dream Weavers is another business venture I'm exploring with my niece, who is also a seamstress. Its focus is on all kinds of things that help people to dream. We're looking at ideas and products now. For example, dream catchers. We also want to make herbal dream pillows like ones they used to make in Europe. I think the possibilities are exciting. After all, people need their dreams in a world as troubled as this one.

A Labor in Gold

Kate Shaw

> If you've always taken care of everybody around you and
> worried about what they needed and how to help them,
> at some point...you've got to ask what makes you happy.
> I don't think I've answered these questions, but I've asked
> them. I'm asking.

Women in the helping professions frequently find it hard to consider their own needs, especially when their professional dedication is matched by a strong ethical dedication to service.

But at some point in their middle years, these women often begin to feel nagged by a need to shift their focus to themselves, to take stock of who they are, to re-define themselves. A period of intense self-questioning—seemingly without satisfactory answers—may be the first signal of this midlife change.

Kate Shaw is an example of a midlife woman who, having committed herself to working on behalf of others for more than twenty-five years, is just now beginning to ask herself what she wants from life. Kate is a soft blonde with dark blue eyes and wonderfully clear skin. She looks as though she could have been her high school's prettiest, most popular cheerleader.

At forty-eight, Kate is a local union president with more than two decades of experience as a union representative in her hometown's specialty pottery of over three hundred employees. She has also raised three children in a difficult marriage situation.

In spite of her ability to stand up for the rights of others in her career, she openly admits to her failure to stand up for her rights within her marriage. She isn't sure about the reasons for this failure, but she continues to look for answers by talking with other women in similar situations. Because her children are now independent adults, she has allowed herself to try some new options.

A brush with cancer and a hysterectomy three years ago have also pushed Kate to begin thinking about her own future. She is dealing with some physical manifestations of aging, and she recognizes the toll on her energy that her work has cost.

While Kate hasn't yet come up with any comfortable answers about what she wants to do for herself, she has a conviction that, at this point, what is important is to keep asking questions.

Kate Shaw

I was born and raised in this town. My father was a steel worker, my mother stayed at home, and my grandparents were potters. Mostly hillbillies.

I got married when I was eighteen, right out of high school. I thought I was madly in love. My future husband went into the military, and he came home and we got married. That was in '62. I conceived my second son when he came home from the Azores one time.

In '68 I had my daughter, and I went to work at the pottery when she was a year old. My mother lived with us and watched my children. In the beginning, I worked in the decorating room, then I worked in the lining department. I've been there for twenty-three years. After the pottery is decorated and glazed, I line it with gold with a small hand paintbrush. I've been lining by hand since '79, anything that needs gold, like gravy boats, special stuff that other potteries don't have.

When my husband got out of the military, he had a couple of different jobs and started college. Then he decided to quit working to go to college full-time. He had pretty much a good time while I was working. He would drive girls from town to the branch campus. I had a lot of rocky years with him running around and all that.

I got involved in the union in my first or second year at the pottery. I didn't seem to have problems taking care of myself, but I didn't like how other people were being treated around me, so I became a shop steward, a union representative that takes care of people's grievances and problems.

My grandmother worked in the pottery here all her life. Everybody's parents worked there, so I was in and out of here all my life. I was real familiar with the pottery and real familiar with times that were bad and times that were good. When they were working good, my grandmother made decent money for back then. But then they would send the people home in the middle of the day, shut down just like that.

My grandmother lived down the road from our house, and she would always stop to see us on her way home. I was familiar with the workings of the pottery, and I was familiar with how strong my grandmother was. I guess it was just in my blood to take care of the people because I knew long years ago how they had been taken care of. I just had that outlook when I got there.

When I became shop steward, I was twenty-three. I was pretty mouthy. And I was so radical back then. These days, you can't legally strike unless it's contract time. Back then you could pretty well walk out any time, and it happened frequently.

We had this one duty in our department that was much more difficult than the rest, this awful machine that was supposed to take steel bits off automatically. But the machine didn't work properly, so the bits were still on, and you had to get them knocked off by hand. It was pretty difficult because that stuff would get in your eyes, so we decided we would take turns every two hours doing it.

The company decided we were being mouthy and cute. They said we had to take five-hour turns, so we walked out. I told the people that we weren't just going to walk out, we would march back and forth through the plant, so everybody would know for sure that we were walking out. We didn't want any doubt in anybody's mind. I would never do that now, but back then I was that radical. It did pretty well straighten management up, though.

When my kids were twelve or thirteen, I got away from being shop steward for a few years. I had my hands full with baseball and football and all that kind of stuff. Then I went from being a machine liner to a gold hand liner, and the people in that department wanted to go on piece work. One of the older women in the department said she didn't want to go on piece work unless someone represented her who she could trust, so I was sort of shoved back into the union stuff.

In '88, I became vice-president of the union. I worked with the woman who had been president for eighteen or nineteen years. We worked really well together. I learned everything I knew, good or bad, from her. Last year, we were still pretty close and everything, and an election was coming up. I had made up my mind that we were still going to run together. But the people weren't satisfied with her. They told me that, if I didn't run for president, they would run four people against her, which would mean you wouldn't have any idea of who would come out as president.

I told her the situation. And she said, "Let the chips fall where they may." I told her I didn't think I could do that. I was pretty frank with her. Well, I did run for president in the election, and I won. She didn't speak to me for awhile, but now she's pretty much back to normal.

Now I'm learning a whole new way of taking care of people. I've taken classes in labor management through the university. I had to go to schooling to learn about workman's comp for the AFL-CIO. I've had to learn things about the Labor Department and OSHA and Health and Welfare and Social

Security, just a variety of things you might come in contact with when you help people.

Even though I've been involved with the union for years, as a new president, management want to see how far they can push me. I think they would basically like to break the union, which a lot of companies are trying to do today anyhow. They want to go back to minimum wage, I'm sure.

You just decide that you can't let management walk on you. It drains you fast. You maybe have one or two pottery workers who are strong with you, but the rest are scared. They just go to union meetings so they can say they do. It's a strain on you, especially as union president, because the workers don't want to talk to you at the pottery because they're scared. So you're like a doctor, you're on duty twenty-four hours of the day because when you're at home, you're still getting calls.

I don't know how people do it, especially a woman because, if you have a family, you're taking care of them, too. Men are a lot more chicken than you realize when you work with them everyday in situations of fear. I've never worked with any man that you take into an office meeting that doesn't panic. I don't know why that is, but they sucker in and do what they're told. They're not good at it.

Something I ought to touch on that I wonder about a lot. The former president of the union, she helped a lot of people, and there's been as many as 350 people at the pottery, so she's helped a lot of people. Her family life and my family life are pretty much the same. Her and I are both real outgoing and take care of everybody else, but both of our basic home lives are the same. Her husband is very spoiled and self-centered, and she in her home and me in my home are completely different from what we are in public. Because we have both taken a lot of crap at home. She's babied him and put up with him. Both of our husbands have gone out drinking and partying and everything. It amazes me how much you put up with in your personal life that you would not allow anyone else to do. I wonder how many women are like that in public who are real outgoing and take care of other people and mouth off, but basically put up with anything at home.

I did get a divorce finally in '80. I didn't date anybody for five years, and then I met another union president at a convention. He was a real soft, sweet man. He didn't think I could do a thing wrong. He wouldn't even believe my girlfriend when she told him I swore. He was really good for my life because I'd never met anybody like that.

But I still didn't feel comfortable. I'd just had too many years with my ex-husband, so we went back together, and he's still exactly the same as he always was, he's no nicer or anything. I don't know why women do dumb things like that. I really don't.

We're not remarried. I haven't gone that far yet. We've been back together about four years. I don't think I could push myself into marriage. He really likes to control. He used to be nasty and slap me years ago when we were married. He wouldn't do that now. He's a little bit afraid of me, but he still talks big.

I've started thinking about myself now. My kids aren't dependent, they're in their twenties. For a lot of years, even though they did pretty well in school, if anything went wrong, they said it was my fault. Because I was there. Because I stayed with their dad. I kept thinking, I stayed with your dad because I wanted you to have a dad. But I basically listened to them. I listened to that crap. Now I crack up and say, "Yeah, right. You guys either make it or you don't make it. I'm living for me now."

What I do for myself now—I have thoughts more than anything. I stay at home a lot still because I'm pretty well tied to him. I'm a homebody. I don't like cooking and cleaning and all that, but I still enjoy being at home.

I think I've had what you call a midlife crisis. In '89, I had a pap test and found out I had cancer. I had a hysterectomy. Once you've had that, you have so many changes. They say you don't gain weight, but you do. And you don't care as much about sex and things like that as you did before. And you feel you're getting older.

I don't know whether you want to blame everything on the hysterectomy, or if at the same time you have a hysterectomy you're changing anyhow. But there's been lots of changes for me. Like with skin—it dries out and gets scaly. I gained twenty pounds, the last fifteen pounds in the last six or seven months.

When you get older and your kids are grown, you've got to start thinking in all reality about death. So at some point, you also have to start thinking about, "Why not let it be my time to start living for myself?"

If you've always taken care of everybody around you and worried about what they needed and how to help them, at some point you think, "Well, if maybe I'm going to live alone for a few years, what am I going to do to make myself happy for the years that maybe nobody is going to take care of me?" I think everybody if they have any intelligence at all gets to this point. You've got to ask what makes you happy.

I don't think I've answered these questions, but I've asked them. I'm asking. I have a hard time trying to take care of just myself. I'll go home at night and I'll say to myself, "Now come on, one day a week you don't have to answer that damn phone. You're not on twenty-four-hour call." I keep talking to myself about taking care of myself and doing what I want to do. But I sort of slide back into the other. I'm not through that part just yet.

I should pretty well know a lot at my age. But now, even though I look older in the mirror, I still feel like running and skipping and jumping on a bike. I still feel real young, but I have to realize that I'm not. I don't know at what point you realize that you're all grown up. At what age you feel all grown older. Women seem to take a long time to get it together. My goal is age fifty-five. I'm not there yet.

Jade and Armor

Lora Jo Foo

> The experience of being out in nature for me is magnified
> because of my childhood. Everything that I associated
> with peace and carefreeness was in the woods or by the
> water, so, now when I'm out there, it's like everything
> gets lifted up...there's a spirituality.

*In Lora's dream, a large, naked Chinese woman appears before her. The woman
has just undergone surgery in Hong Kong to replace her hip, shoulder, and collar-
bones with ancient jade. Apparently, she has just helped Lora in some emergency,
and now, tired from exerting herself physically, she needs to rest. Lora sees that the
woman is very strong and solid; she also sees the woman's fragile jade bones.*

*Lora asks her, "Can't you stay in the U.S. if you want to?" And the woman
responds, "I belong to Koret [a garment manufacturing corporation] of California."*

Lora Jo Foo (her real name) is a forty-one-year-old litigation attorney special-
izing in employment/labor law at the Asian Law Caucus in San Francisco. Her
dream of the jade woman occurred almost two years ago when Lora was beginning
what she now describes as a midlife crisis.

Lora recorded this dream in her journal. For her, the dream represents a surprising connection to her Chinese heritage that she had believed was minimal because she grew up in the Westernized world.

The dream may have even more significance. The Chinese woman's story is
much like Lora's. For the last twenty years, Lora has dedicated herself first as a
union organizer and now as an attorney to protecting the rights of Asian immi-
grants in their struggle for decent wages and working conditions (in fact, she was a
shop steward at Koret). The hard work took its toll when Lora's body started to
rebel, to break down in ways that demanded her attention. Her emotions, which
she had buried for many years, partly because of her political commitment, unex-
pectedly began to surface.

Overwhelmed both physically and emotionally, Lora took a leave of absence from her job. She regained her health and sought out ways of strengthening her body. In therapy, she explored the implications of her childhood on the adult she has become. She has made a commitment to take care of herself by putting limits on her work week.

Another consequence of Lora's crisis is that she has re-discovered her childhood love of nature and become seriously involved in nature photography. Her photographs of desert, sea, trees, and mountains demonstrate that she has a sure talent for capturing the rich faces of nature. Beneath the beauty of photographs like those titled "Heart Tree" and "Mother Earth" are evocative messages about the universal potential for tranquility, love, strength, and new beginnings.

Lora Jo Foo

I was one of six daughters born in a family in the inner-city ghetto of San Francisco's Chinatown. My childhood years were claustrophobic. There were eight of us living in federal housing in the second most crowded community in the United States.

I went to school nine months out of the year and worked in the garment factory in the summer months starting when I was eleven. I worked with my mother. We sat behind sewing machines to earn the money we needed to pay the rent and put food on the table. Sometimes, during the school year, I worked on weekends, too, but I had to get my homework done first.

The next summer, the summer of '63, I again went to work for eleven hours a day, six days a week. Only that summer, my church sent me off to summer camp for one week. For one wonderful week, I played games like other children, went swimming in the Russian River, hiked, gossiped about boys, and I had no responsibilities other than being a child. The week ended quickly. Then I was back in the sweatshop.

If the sweatshop had been windowless or had drapes over the doors and windows like so many of the others did, I wouldn't have been so miserable. Instead, this factory had windows facing a tree-lined parking lot. I could hear the birds singing and feel the occasional breeze. I could imagine the sunshine on my skin through the open windows. At age twelve, I felt caged and trapped and powerless.

I felt this way even at home. I felt the powerlessness of being used. My mother used to say to us, "Don't let your father treat you like a girl-child slave." I would go to lots of Chinese movies with my mother. Usually, they were about a wealthy family who somehow lost their wealth and sold off the daughter as a slave to another family.

And so my mother used to say, "Don't let him treat you like a girl-child slave. If you were in China, he would have sold you a long time ago for money." She used to say that to us when we were seven, eight, nine years old. Basically, my association with being a girl and a child is with being a slave.

When I got to age fourteen, I rebelled, I refused to work anymore. I became a teenager for a little while. I became very defiant with my father.

One day, when I was sixteen, I was riding home from school on the bus, and, on Stockton Street, I saw this picket line of Chinese immigrant women in their thirties and forties and fifties. They were unionizing a fashion designer's sweatshop, marching around with picket signs.

I looked at that picket line, and I had this exhilarating feeling about oppressed Asian women standing up for themselves. I got so excited. The next day, I went into the high school cafeteria and gave my first political speech, convincing people to come out and support those women on the picket line. In my mind, a union was a safe haven, a safe haven for girl-child slaves and oppressed immigrant women.

But before I really became political, I made my living as an artist. I became a fashion designer for a little while during the late '60s, during the hippie era when San Francisco was the center of everything. I went to fashion design school for six months, and I picked up enough to be able to design, to become a pattern maker.

One of my clients said, "Why don't you start manufacturing your designs?" I was doing men's leather and velveteen shirts at that point. My client wanted to set me up in business, so he sent me into a fashion designer's shop. Actually, it was the same shop that I had seen the Asian women picket a couple of years earlier.

I walked into that shop, and I looked around, and I said, "I'm going to become a boss? I'm going to become a manufacturer? I'm going to have to hire a group of women and try to pay them minimum wage?" I didn't do it. That ended my life as an artist for the next twenty years. I was nineteen then, and I needed to escape to the woods.

After a summer of working in the canneries in Alaska, I came back home and immediately got into community organizing. The Asian-American Studies Program at San Francisco State University was recruiting students, so I also became a college student. In the last semester of my senior year, though, I decided I had had enough of academia. It was time to go back to the real world.

That's when I went back into the sewing factory. It was a union shop, and I became shop steward. I also worked in a hotel as a maid, cleaning rooms and toilets. My political life took off in earnest. I became consumed with politics for the next eight years. On top of the really hard manual labor was all the evenings of meetings and strategy planning and fighting with union bureaucrats. We worked with a reform slate to eventually take over a union, and we went on strike for the first time in forty years in the hotel union.

I got married in 1979. We had lived together for four years before that, so, as far as I'm concerned, we've been married since '75. For a little while, we were doing political work together. We were comrades-in-arms. But then, he started cutting back, exploring other interests like classical music. I was still very absorbed in the union organizing.

When I added up all of the intense union work I had been doing for eight years, I knew I was wearing my body down. I decided it was time for a reprieve. I wanted to go to law school, so I went back and finished off the last semester of college and went to law school from there. I thought it would be easier, and it was. It was easier being an intellectual than leading six thousand workers on strike.

Unfortunately, I wasn't reading the continuing signs of my body's deterioration. I was just pushing, mind over matter. I was really feeling tired. When I went backpacking, I got nauseated on the trail, and, at that point, I should have known I had already pushed my body to the brink. But I just kept going on. You think the body will stay young forever, but it doesn't—especially if you don't take care of it.

After law school, I knew I didn't want to commit myself in the same way to union organizing, but I couldn't get out of the save-the-world mode. Instead, I went from law school into a law firm that represented unions up and down California. This firm has the reputation of being the toughest, meanest labor law firm in the country.

I did try to pull myself back. I chose what I thought was an easier route—doing pension and trust fund work—with just a little bit of the traditional union stuff. But it doesn't matter what area of the law you work in, you just end up working like a dog anyway.

After three years of that, I started going through more physical symptoms of stress, like dry heaves. My hormones were completely out of whack. My body wasn't holding the uterine lining anymore, so that, in between menstrual periods, I would keep having these drips that went on and on. Those were the physical signs. Then there were the emotional signs. Because of my childhood, I had this armor encasing my entire body to protect me from the rest of the world. I was in total control of my life and had never cried in front of anybody—never—not even as a child except for once with my best friend. But the armor was beginning to crack. One day, I had this confrontation with the managing partner of the law firm. My voice started cracking, and I knew I was going to cry, so I just stood up and left his office and went into the bathroom and broke down. I'd never done that in my entire life. I knew something was wrong.

About this time, I started taking Model Mugging classes. Model Mugging is a self-defense class where groups of women teach other women how to defend themselves. It's called Model Mugging because they have a mugger who is fully padded and protected, and he comes at you full force. You learn how to defend yourself from a position of being on the ground; the idea is that, when a man attacks a woman, he takes the woman down to the ground. You learn to defend yourself with your legs because, for women, your legs are always stronger than your upper part. The course is one of those experiences that, once you go through it, you never forget. It's part of your body.

Many of the women who take the classes are rape and incest survivors, and, when there is an attack on someone who is a survivor and she successfully defends herself, sometimes that woman breaks down and cries. When this happens, everybody sits down together, and there's a lot of hugging. In this group, I realized it was okay to cry, and I asked myself why I hadn't done it for twenty years. Why had I repressed it?

After that, I decided to go to psychotherapy. In my culture, psychotherapy is just not something people do. Given my political background, the touchy-feely part of life was not correct either. I had to face a bunch of hurdles before I finally got myself to therapy.

Fortunately, I had a hardhitting therapist who didn't mince words. He saw I was deteriorating, ruining my body, and he had a hard time getting me to stop what I was doing. Finally, he asked me, "If you had a dog, would you treat your dog this way? Isn't this cruelty to animals what you're doing to your body?" His question stopped me. That was the only way I could see it. I couldn't see it in terms of myself, but I could see it in terms of the suffering of somebody else.

I had what I would call a midlife crisis. Basically, it was a breakdown, my body rebelling, just refusing to do it anymore. I decided it was time to take care of myself, and I asked for six months off from the office. They agreed to it. I ended up taking eight months off. I started trying to figure out what it is I want to do with the second half of my life.

I started getting my health back together again and doing the things that I wanted to do when I was young but just put aside. I started biking and backpacking again. This is also about the time that I got into nature photography.

I went back to the law firm and worked a three-day week. That worked for about nine months, but then the position in the Asian Law Caucus opened up last January. I asked them if they were willing to hire me on a three-day week. In the end, I went in on a five-day week, but I said I'd only work nine to five.

Well, that's not working. It's not possible. I'm the only employment/ labor attorney representing low income Asian-American workers for seven counties. There's no other pro bono attorney concentrating just on the Asian community. But I've been negotiating. I've actually said that, as much as I like this job, my health comes first. They're taking it seriously. They don't want to lose me, so they're trying to figure something out short of hiring another attorney because there's no money for another one.

I know why it's been so hard for me to pull away. When I look at myself as a girl-child slave, when I look at my mother as an oppressed garment worker, when I look at immigrant women all over who are working long hours and for low wages, I know that their relief will come through unionization. In an organizing drive, no one gives you your freedom. You stand up for yourself and do something about your life.

I've decided that, in the second half of my life, I really do want to continue contributing, but I'm paying attention to my body. I'm no longer shuffling it into the background. At least, now, I'm conscious of why I'm so drawn to the labor movement, and that helps a little bit in terms of pulling back.

I may have to leave the law altogether. See if there's some other way of contributing without having to work that way. I see myself heading in that direction slowly, but I just can't make the break immediately. I'm just seeing the progression. I need something interesting and challenging that doesn't burn me out. There's not that many jobs like that around.

Nature photography I love. I squeeze in at least one morning a week to go to the darkroom. And every couple of months or so, I take off to the Sierra Nevada or Yosemite Valley or the desert. Maybe I'll go back to being an artist. I enjoyed that period. I enjoyed the solitude. But it's much tougher now making a living as an artist than it was back then.

The experience of being out in nature for me is magnified because of my childhood experience. Everything that I associated with peace and carefreeness was in the woods or by the water, so, now when I'm out there, it's like everything gets lifted up. The burden gets lifted. There's a spirituality. I'm amazed at the things I see.

I've figured out that I'm drawn subconsciously to photographing certain things. When I print a picture, I look at it and look at it, and I wonder what drew me to it. And then I realize themes come and go, just like themes in dreams.

For a while, I was taking pictures of trees growing out of rocks. Trees that survive in harsh settings. I just kept taking these pictures, and one day I realized why I was so attracted to these trees. It was my background, surviving it. Once I realized that, I stopped taking those types of pictures and moved on to other themes. I think my photography tells the story of my life.

My marriage almost ended in divorce about two years ago when I started going through all these changes. My husband and I loved each other, but what had kept us together through the years was that we were comrades-in-arms.

When I started going though therapy and my feelings started coming out, then I wanted to have a relationship that had passion in it and romance. It took him awhile to adjust, but, because he loved me enough and wanted our relationship to work, he decided to try it. He's funny about it, but he's trying hard enough for me to say, okay, I'm satisfied. And he's changing in the process. We're both changing and staying together.

Peace Elder and Sundancer

Mary Elizabeth Thunder

> Before my heart attack, I think my whole life was geared
> to killing myself. The heart attack gave me courage to
> change. And now my life is geared to life, beauty, joy,
> celebration, creating that which helps other people. Any-
> one who dreams to do this can do this.

*Part Cheyenne, Mohawk, adopted Lakota Sioux, and Irish, Mary Elizabeth Thun-
der (her real name) is a short, heavily built woman with gentle brown eyes and a
soft voice. She is a forty-eight-year-old Lakota peace elder dedicated to a life of
teaching and ministering to the spiritual needs of people. In 1989, at the request of
the elders of several Indian nations and in response to a spirit vision she had in
1982, she established Thunder-Horse Ranch, a "spiritual university," in West
Point, Texas. People of many religious faiths come to this ranch to pray for personal and world peace and to participate in traditional Indian ceremonies.*

*Thunder's acceptance of her role as a teacher started dramatically in 1981
when she suffered a heart attack and had a near-death experience. Before then, she
had spent her adult life alternately trying to cope with and deny the abuse she
experienced in her childhood.*

*The heart attack allowed Thunder to let go of the anger and pain she had
carried for so many years. Recognizing the rich spirituality of her Native American
roots, she turned to the elders for guidance on how to create a new, meaningful life.
As often happens when a woman taps into her potential, the result has been synergistic: Thunder became a teacher, a sun dancer, then a peace elder. She created the
ranch. In the process of this growth, she has also been able to heal the wounds in her
immediate family.*

*The source of Thunder's strength lies in her Native American heritage. For
example, she is a veteran of twenty sun dances, a difficult ritual that forces its
participants to assess and deal with both their fears and their abilities as well as to
acknowledge the power of the Great Spirit. Thunder has also been mentored by
elders like Mary Crow Dog, Grace Spotted Eagle and Twylah Nitsch, women*

who have been acknowledged for their wisdom far beyond indigenous communities. In her turn, Thunder has become a teacher and healer to many people.

Our interview takes place when Thunder's family, friends, and students as well as many elders have gathered at the ranch to celebrate the New Year rituals. Forced indoors by heavy rains, people are cooking, eating, laughing, playing games, talking, discussing ceremonies.

In the middle of all this activity, Thunder sits in a flowered easy chair and talks about the changes in her life. As the head of this ranch, she is clearly a woman facing many responsibilities and challenges. But what impresses us most is her openness and sense of peace.

Mary Elizabeth Thunder

I was an only child, born in Indianapolis. My mother and father were both part Indian. My mother deserted me at three weeks, and I went through foster homes until I was about three. And then I went back to my father's home—well, that made me ready to go back to a foster home.

I was an exceedingly precocious child with an IQ of 171. At one or two, I was on the radio reciting "The Night Before Christmas." That was part of me, and then there was the other part that was being violated every second of every day at home.

My father sexually abused me, and I hated him for years. I believe I dealt with this by becoming split off. There was the working Mary, and there was the go-to-college Mary, and later there was the wife Mary and the mother Mary. I had all these parts that never integrated. I was totally dysfunctional. That's why I studied psychology at Indiana University—to figure myself out. I have studied a lot of therapies—psychodrama, TA, TM, you name it—all this stuff to find the peace of a whole person.

Unknowingly, I became semi-abusive as a parent, modeling what I had learned. I had no other references. I started studying Indian ways to get my family back together. That's what first got me studying my heritage—a hope for some answers in Indian culture on how to live in harmony. I would travel from Indiana to South Dakota with my family just to go to a ceremony to try to bring us all back together.

In 1981, when I was working as an assistant to the mayor of Indianapolis, I had a heart attack and died on the operating table. I had a near-death experience of much beauty and serenity and peace. I didn't want to come back, but the Spirits told me I had something to do.

Leonard Crow Dog, a Lakota elder, had prophesied the heart attack, the death experience, and the visit to the spirit world, and he said I would become a sun dancer. One week to the day after he told me that, I had the heart attack.

When I finally woke up, I got very serious. I was ready. Death was not the big fear any more. Transcending pain, pain's our big stopper. We all work so hard not to be in pain that we'll do anything. We'll stay years and years and years in a painful situation, so we won't have to face the pain of change.

The elders, Leonard and Mary Crow Dog, Wallace Black Elk, Grace Spotted Eagle and others, counseled me about what to do. The first thing they said was that I would go on the road as a teacher. They also said I would have students. I laughed and asked, "So what am I supposed to teach them?" I didn't think I had anything to share with anybody. Grandma Grace Spotted Eagle, one of the elders, said, "You're going to teach students what you need to know."

I said, "Okay, how am I going to recruit these students? Where am I supposed to get these enlightened individuals who are going to follow a woman who doesn't know where she's going?" They told me to follow the Sacred Pipe, to believe in the guidance of the Spirit. They told me I should give up my house and everything to go on the road to teach. And then these wonderful people just started showing up wherever I went, and I've been teaching them what I need to know ever since. It's been amazing. I was on the road teaching for nine years out of a van.

I had been adopted by Henry and Mary Crow Dog in 1974. Henry really, truly believed as much as he could in an environment that would be peaceful for all races. He believed that all races would come together to dance. Because of prejudice, he would say, this will be a long time coming, but it will come. We will do it. Before my heart attack, I think my whole life was geared to killing myself. The heart attack gave me courage to change. And now my life is geared to life, beauty, joy, celebration, creating that which helps other people. Anyone who dreams to do this can do this.

When I was forty, I came to the realization that I should honor my father just for giving me life—nothing more was necessary. I had worked for years to get to this point. My father was really domineering schizophrenic so I couldn't even be in a room with him for maybe ten minutes before he would explode and hit me or shoot a gun at me or something.

I spent my whole life trying to change him. I know he's why I got into the work I did originally—human rights, loving people —because he hated everybody. I went out to prove him wrong, and, in doing so, he became my greatest teacher. He was actually my greatest energy source for teaching.

He passed on about a year ago. By the time he died, we had healed together, and we actually were able to sit in a room together and laugh and feel neat together. He made it possible for me to walk my talk, to put into action what I taught. I reclaimed the father, and he reclaimed the daughter before he passed on.

I don't believe that, in the early years of my children's lives, I was a good mother. I was a loving mother, a playful mother, but I didn't discipline well. I was ignorant and continually re-creating familiar pain from my own childhood. My kids told me what to do, my husband told me what to do, everybody in the world told me what to do. I had no concept of taking control for myself.

After the Spirit helped me walk through my fears and grow, I realized that, in order to heal the family of the world, I had to go back and atone for the things I did in my core family. I started therapy with all of my children. I realized that they were keeping this same dysfunctionality alive in their own families.

I never told my children that what I did was wrong. All I said was, "I know your life has been painful. And forgive me. Now, what can we do?" Watching your children live in this pain is real hard. Just going in and not judging them and not trying to force them to change—just being there where they are has been very difficult.

One year after my heart attack, I started sun dancing at Leonard and Mary Crow Dog's. I was one of the first women half-breeds to do this. It's a dance of many extremes. Because I needed that extreme in my life, that's what I did.

As a sun dancer, you dance for four days and four nights with no food and no water, usually in temperatures above a hundred degrees and often at high elevations. The sun dance is primarily a Plains Indians ritual for renewal of the earth. It's the masculine principle of the sun being in connection with the feminine principle of the earth. The dancers make prayers for peace so that people may live.

The sun dance has taught me many, many lessons. One of the lessons is that what I feared would happen in the dance would usually manifest for me. If I feared falling down, for example, it would happen. If I feared others yelling at me, they would. As I worked through and healed pieces of myself, I was able to help others. You have to watch your thoughts because they create your reality.

You learn in the sun dance the lesson that you are not in control of this planet. You are not God. In fact, you are nothing. I'm not this spiffy little jogging person. During the dance, when I have heart pains again, when I call out to a higher power, something greater, the Great Mystery, *Tunka Shila*, I get an answer. The Spirit renews my energy, gives me the strength to go on. I could be down in the dirt, crying in the dirt, "Please help me, help me. Someone or something's going to have to help me." A power more powerful than I must handle this—God.

The minute I do this, then I get the energy, water comes to my mouth, and I go on. I dance usually about two or three times a year, and I have a lot of fear when I'm getting ready to start. I keep thinking I'm too old to do this.

You have to get help from the Creator. Put your head up, put your arms up and pray. This is the way life is. This is the lesson we all have to learn. You must call forth your own energy and strength by calling to the Spirit.

Four years ago, Elder Charles Chipps asked me to take the first position ever of a woman helper in a sun dance. They had never had a reference point for women to do this before. It has been so hard, but I feel I have helped make way for other women to come forth.

In the early days, a long time ago, families, tribes, and clans had a woman leader. She gave birth, she was the initiator of creativity, she was the movement of beauty and tranquility within the structure. She kept the harmony. It was White Buffalo Woman who brought the Sacred Pipe to the Sioux. We got very much away from the idea of women's power, but now it is coming back.

Last year at the sun dance, Leonard Crow Dog said that the feminine has risen, it is here. I'm very concerned about what this means for women. When I walk into the sun dance as mother of the dance, I think about how I'm going to do this, what my role is. Probably, some men resent me, think they will all die because I'm there. But I am there for all the people—men and women.

Women need to learn their power, their importance, and go into themselves to look for this if they have no role models. Women need to be in touch with Spirit and with each other. They need to work together and pray together.

I have been lucky to have some role models. Grace Spotted Eagle was a model for me. She taught me how to accept from people, which was very hard for me coming from my background. But given the life I have chosen, I have to accept from people, from my students. Grandma Twylah Nitsch is also my role model. I follow these leaders. This gives me peace in my heart. Having a woman as an elder and respecting her is so important.

Leonard and Mary Crow Dog named me Thunder. I thought it was because I was quite heavy, some three hundred pounds, and I snored very loudly. I thought the name was a joke. It was embarrassing. But then Leonard told me that Thunder brought out the fact that I am really in communication with Spirit.

When I divorced my first husband, I wanted to take on the energy of my spiritual ways—not the energy of being a daughter or a wife, and not the energy of the today world—I retained my first given names, Mary Elizabeth, and changed my last name to Thunder in the court. The elders gave me permission to do this.

I was married for twenty-three years, and I said when I got my divorce that I would never remarry. I was too dysfunctional. I thought, "I'll just pray. I like to pray. I'll walk alone. I can't deal with relationships." The elders had other ideas about that.

I remember Grandma Grace Spotted Eagle saying, "But a woman cannot be alone, a man cannot be alone. You're born into this world as a part of something and, when you find the other part, that becomes a whole." I asked, "But what if you are always fighting the other half and that becomes your life's work?"

Horse came on the road in 1985. I hated him from the moment I saw him. He was irritating and young, nineteen years younger than me. Sickeningly sweet. He loved everything. Nobody loves everything. I thought, "Where did he come from and who does he think he is?" Grandma Grace thought I should take him with me on the road. She thought I needed him. I told her I didn't need him. I liked to fight in those days.

It turned out later that I did need him as a driver. We were together on the road for five years. When his father passed on, I realized...Grandma called and asked why I wasn't at his side. She said I loved him. I said, "Yeah, but..." I went into all the problems it could create. She said it was okay. I should be by his side because he needed me. She gave her blessings on the wedding even though she didn't live to see it. All the elders advised that he would have a softening effect on my hardness. They were right. We've been married since 1989. I'm not anything like I used to be. I'm very soft now. I'm still a warrior, but I'm soft.

A New York film director came to the first Peace Elders gathering. She came to meet with Grandma Twylah and me. The director asked if Horse was really my husband. I told her he was. Grandma asked her why she asked in that tone. She said, "Well, he's good looking and so much younger."

Then the director asked me, "Don't you ever worry about him leaving you?" Grandma answered for me: "Her worry about him leaving her? Ha! He needs to worry every day, every minute that this powerful woman will leave him. She could have any man in the world, and she chose him."

After nine years of teaching on the road, we bought this land in Texas and started Thunder-Horse Ranch. That was 1989. I had seen this place in a vision in 1983. We even have a buffalo now, Star Keeper, a gift from a sun dance chief.

The Spirit said this ranch would be a survival camp in the sense that we need to work through our emotional junk and move on. This is the age of Aquarius, when, as the song says, peace will rule the planet and love will guide us all. We put love in action here. That's important. Ministering to the people. This is a spiritual university; it's for all faiths, not just Native Americans. I live the Lakota life, but even Tibetan lamas have come here to pray. I have been blessed by the Dalai Lama.

We're just getting started. Toxic waste is one of the problems of the planet; even worse are toxic thoughts. We work through these thoughts in rituals, like the sweat lodge that purifies the body, the mind, the spirit. This land is teaching emotional survival to help bring more harmony on the planet.

The second Peace Elder Conference, Wolf Song II, was here on the ranch in May, 1992. More than seventy indigenous elders from all over the world came. We built a teaching lodge for the elders dedicated to the preservation of the teachings and ceremonial ways of life of all indigenous peoples. The conference itself was dedicated to change. Change is what gives us our growth.

Service is an important part of my life. I get up in the morning and ask how can I be of service today? I don't have a schedule. That's just how we live.

Putting the Pieces Together

Lee Robertson

> You do die. You die to the false self, and you are re-
> created. At first, it frightened me to be alone to do
> this....It is scary, but, if you can get to the other side, you
> see a promise and great hope there.

*Sometimes a need for change presents itself initially as a vague but nagging dissat-
isfaction. This is how Lee, a fifty-year-old New Englander, began her midlife
evolution.*

*When she began to make plans in her mid-forties for retirement, Lee had to
confront a vague inner sense of not being "in the right place" that had plagued her
all her adult life. She responded to these feelings by asking questions about the
purpose and meaning of her life.*

*In her willingness to struggle through these issues, Lee experienced an unfold-
ing of her identity. Counseling and prayer yielded insight and guidance in her quest
for wholeness.*

*Her new commitment to solitude also allowed her time to become comfortable
with emerging parts of her self. As she grew in self-understanding and spiritual
awareness, she became more integrated and free to live a more authentic life.*

*A mutual friend brings us to Lee's home where we are immediately welcomed
into her small kitchen. Light pours through the window onto a collection of healthy-
looking ferns.*

*Lee is a gregarious and hospitable woman. By the time the interview begins,
we are joking, and Lee's hearty laughter fills the room.*

Lee Robertson

I was the older of two children. My younger sister and I got along great. My mother had a very strong personality and was a strict disciplinarian. My father was much more laid back.

School was a real source of aggravation for me because I didn't do well. It's only been late in my life that I have been able to understand why I couldn't do better. My mother was so powerful and so strong, and this was one of the ways I had of telling her, "You can't make me." You can't make someone get good grades. But not doing well in school was a stigma I carried for many years, even as an adult.

I went to work for the electric company when I was eighteen. We have a family tradition of people working in the electric company. My grandmother retired from there. I came up through the rank and file and was quite successful in my career. But still, I never quite felt adequate because I had done poorly in school. One reason I later wanted to return to school was to prove to myself that I could do it.

My family went to a Methodist church, but we weren't what I would call a religious family. You would go if the spirit moved you or wouldn't go if the spirit didn't. Of if you had been out late, that kind of thing.

About ten years ago, I started going back to church periodically and was asked to be on the search committee for a new associate pastor. The pastor we called became a very good friend of mine. Although she was about thirteen years younger than me, she became a role model in that she had worked her way through seminary. She introduced me to spirituality, which, to me, means the personal relationship we have with God.

For all the thirty years that I worked at the electric company, there was always a part of me that never felt I was quite in the right place. I was always placed in jobs that had nothing to do with my creative side. They never were exactly what I wanted to do. There were certainly parts of my career that I enjoyed, but there was always this piece of me that never felt quite right.

After I met this friend from church, we spent a lot of time talking about God and reading many different books about spirituality. I decided that I really needed to do something new with my life. I kept asking myself, "What is my purpose for being? Why am I here?" I had all the things that society says you need. I had a sports car. I had a house. I had money. I traveled. I did all the things everybody thinks they want to do. But I didn't feel right. A piece of me said, "There has to be something more than this." A very empty feeling.

Another part of my struggle in my early forties concerned my lack of education. I wanted to go back to school because I wanted to know more about faith, about God. I needed to have a grasp of what it was I really believed. But I was afraid I'd fail because of my past experience with school. One day, I just swallowed hard and picked up the phone and called the admissions office at a local Catholic college. I attended my first theology class in November of 1985.

I had become very involved in my church and thought I was being called to become a minister. When people began to realize I was studying to become a minister, some of them began to talk to me about their faith. I discovered that people like to talk about their beliefs. That was important and encouraging to me. So my last four years at work became a kind of ministry. It was the way I survived there because my heart was really somewhere else.

I retired in 1990. At that time, several important changes took place in my life. Besides retiring, I had a personal loss, a broken relationship, which caused me to take stock of who I was. I decided that I needed professional help, so I began seeing a counselor.

One of the major issues I needed to deal with was my sexuality. It is still amazing to me that you can live a whole lifetime, and part of you can live a lie or not acknowledge who you are. It's like a certain piece of you didn't exist. And you pay a price for it. A dear price.

Once you discover that—once you can look at that—well, I was gay. I denied this piece of who I was for all the usual reasons. I didn't want to be rejected. I certainly didn't want to tell my family. But the bottom line is that there are no good reasons for denying it. In the end, my family was very supportive.

I had lived with a number of different women. And that always bothered me. I wondered why I couldn't have one relationship and make it work. What happened to me in my search was that I started looking at my relationship with my mother. Our relationship had been terrible since I was a child. I discovered that I had lived her life for thirty years, not my own. It has only been in the last three or four years that I have been living my own life. For the first time, I can claim it. It's like getting a whole new skin.

My search helped me to discover that many of my relationships with women were actually a search for what my mother did not give me. Now I'm not sure I've sorted out what side of the fence I'm on as far as my sexuality goes, or that it's really important to me anymore. What I have learned is that my sexuality is just one piece of who I am. For right now, my choice is to live pretty much a celibate life. That is what feels right to me. I'm working toward wholeness now, toward taking all of the pieces of who I am and becoming more whole.

As I understood more about my mother, I wanted us to create a new relationship. I wanted us to redefine what we are for each other, so I prayed about it. One day I stopped by her house and said to her, "We need to do something different." And she said, "Well, I guess maybe I didn't do some things right."

I told her it didn't mean that we couldn't create something new and make things different and better. My mother hates change. But who the hell likes it? I'm not into it either, and I certainly didn't like all the changes that were going on in *my* life.

But one of the things my mother and I had in common was our faith, so, rather than talk about our relationship, we decided we would just say a prayer for each other whenever we were together. We did that for a long period of time. And I can honestly say that today our relationship is different. I think we have both grown. Now she doesn't interfere, she respects my need to make my own decisions.

Often you don't realize how controlled you are by another human being. It is truly frightening the amount of influence and power parents have over their children. She and I have been able to talk about it and about her own childhood, too. I think it is important to do this because our childhood makes a major impact on us as adults. You drag all that stuff with you. Every bit of it! Until it's really looked at, the same mistakes get made all over again, and you can't move toward becoming a whole person.

My counselor helped me understand my relationship with my mother, but she couldn't help me with the spiritual part of who I was. Something was going on with this part of me, and it was very profound.

At this point, my friend from the church left town, and I had quit going there because it was too painful for me. I was looking for another church to attend within my denomination. I had no intentions of becoming a Catholic, but I was taking a class on the Nicean Creed. It was during this time of studying the creed that I developed a very, very deep sense that communion really represented the body and blood of Christ, it wasn't just a symbol. In my church, we believed that communion was pretty much symbolic, but I was coming to have a deep sense that it was much more than symbol.

One day I was in class, sitting there totally absorbed in thinking about the different interpretations of communion and how I felt about them. I was called on to answer a question. I was so out of it that I told the instructor I couldn't answer his question. Then I shared what I had been thinking and feeling with the class. I told them I would never again be able to take communion with the same understanding. I was told that I needed to experience communion in a community that believed it was the real body of Christ. I didn't take that too much to heart at the time.

But for the next four Sundays, I went to four different Methodist churches, and each one served communion. Now in most Methodist churches, communion is only served one Sunday a month. But in every church I picked, they served communion on the Sunday I was there. It was amazing, so much coincidence. I felt like someone was telling me something.

When I finally decided to leave the Methodist church, though, I was feeling very depressed. Not having my church home was a blow. I had already retired from my job, and now I didn't have my church. Friends at the college were very supportive. They listened to me and gave me the guidance I needed. One of them suggested that I should try going to the small Catholic church she went to. I did, and the congregation made me feel very special and very welcome. Now I've been confirmed, and that place is home to me.

One of the most moving experiences I have ever had was the rite of welcoming at my confirmation service. The congregation sang welcoming songs to the people who were going to be confirmed. They read the most beautiful Biblical passages to us and made the sign of the cross on all our senses—our eyes, our mouths, our hands, our feet—repeating these gorgeous words.

It was one of the most profound experiences I have ever had. I looked up once out into the community, and they were all in tears. That church is a powerful place. There is a real mixture of people there—blacks, Hispanics, rich, poor, highly educated, uneducated.

I feel very fortunate. Most people who make these transitions are not in the position I am. They still have jobs they have to go to. But you need time to go into your room and close the door—time to be with yourself. You not only get to know yourself, but you can get to know God. God's not up there. God is in here. [She points to her heart.]

A couple of years ago, I learned to write a journal. At the beginning of the day, I would be by myself and write. And all of the pain I was going through seemed as if it was on the outside of me. But I had a deep sense that there was something on the other side of this. The Psalms were a comfort to me—and the idea of dying and being reborn.

And you do die. You die to the false self, and you are re-created. At first, it frightened me to be alone to do this. I didn't know this new person. It is scary but, if you can get to the other side, you see a promise and great hope there.

I guess I had to get down into the pit before I could work my way out. Maybe it is in the depths of our pain that we begin to know who God is in us. It is my belief that the more we can embrace who we really are and love ourselves, the more we can begin to reach out to others.

So that is my life. Right now is a very peaceful time for me. Nature plays a powerful role in my life now. I see things today in nature that I never even knew were there. I've learned to enjoy the quiet—to look closely at a flower and see what it really looks like. You have to slow down to do that.

I feel a sense now, not of being done, but of having made an inward journey and being ready to go back out into the world.

I now know that I have a gift of really being present to others. People can share with me, and they don't feel threatened. They tell me things that they might not share with someone else. I think part of that is my ability to share who it is that I am. I have learned that, if you dare to risk sharing who you are with another, it lets people feel like they can share themselves, too.

I have decided to use my gift by becoming a pastoral counselor. I feel very clear about this decision. And I go a lot on what feels good. If it doesn't feel right to me, then I don't do it. Your head is a wonderful thing, but it gets in the way sometimes. We have wonderful intuitions and gut feelings to use. This is the way I like to describe how I saw myself before: When I looked in the mirror, I saw this puzzle with all these vacant places. The last few years, I've been filling in the pieces of that face in the puzzle.

Shoes of Many Colors

Maria Vasquez

> It took me forty-four years to realize that all the answers
> aren't going to be settled. Part of me was always looking
> for black and white answers, and I discovered that life is
> just not that way. Now I view life as a process of growth.

A few minutes of conversation with Maria Vasquez reveals a natural and charm-ing innocence that makes one feel at ease and trusting. She is a beautiful woman blessed with classic features; her bright red lipstick enhances her Latin beauty. She is also a pleasure to listen to. Her lilting voice and slight accent strike the ear like music. There is something fresh and brand-new about Maria. And, in a sense, she is brand-new.

Maria grew up in the Southwest, the oldest of four daughters of a traditional Mexican-American, Catholic couple. When she was ten, her parents divorced. Her family's strong religious heritage, however, influenced her choice of a religious vocation after high school. This choice became her identity as well as her vocation. She followed her heart's desire into a cloistered order of nuns.

Almost twenty years later, Maria began questioning everything from her vo-cation to the meaning of spirituality. Eventually, she decided to leave her happy, but restrictive environment to explore what else life had to offer.

In the five years since she left the cloister, Maria has had to focus her energy on many basic identity and survival issues. As many women who married in the 1950s and 1960s romanticized their futures, Maria had a romantic conception of religious life. Many of her experiences seem to fit the pattern of women who divorce after years of marriage.

She has faced the hardship of finding a job with limited marketable skills, expe-rienced the awkwardness of dating and the uncertainties of independent living. Years of relying on others to fulfill her most primary needs ill-prepared her for her new life.

Maria still carries mixed feelings about her past. She recalls the happiness she experienced in contemplative life at the same time she regrets the loss of her youth to the restrictions of that life. As with all of us, no matter how we have chosen, life carries regrets.

Her faith in her ability to cope and her openness to the possibilities for happiness that change can bring have sustained her. At this point in her life, having answered some questions about her basic needs and desires, she is allowing herself to explore more self-fulfilling choices.

As Maria's experience bears out, the way to deal with critical changes is often to simply tough it out. By waiting with some care and patience for the answers that lie within, women gain strength and learn to trust their inner wisdom. In turn, this strength and wisdom open new, sometimes totally unexpected possibilities for personal fulfillment.

Maria Vasquez

My decision to leave the order is something I will have to live with for the rest of my life. Like many other people, I made a major decision early in life, never questioning that I would want to change my commitment.

When I announced to my family that I was joining a religious order, everyone was elated. Except for my mother. It was hard on her when I entered at age nineteen, and it was equally hard on her when I left the order.

The convent had double grilles and curtains separating us from our visitors, so, for many years, I was not able to embrace my mother. Once, when my mother came to visit me, we were in the visiting parlor, and she needed to use the restroom. I rushed to borrow a key to let her in the area where we were. When I opened the grille door to let her in, she tried to hug me. I pulled away because I was taught that was not allowed.

When I look back, I imagine what my mother must have gone through then. I can cry when I think about that. But I was young, and I had this romantic sense of spirituality.

I was one of eleven women sent to Des Moines to begin a new community here. I was twenty-nine years old, and my job was Directress of Novices. My superior was only a couple of years older than me. We came with the idea that we would grow in number. We were taught to measure success by how many people we had. What we came to learn had little to do with numbers.

The experience in religious communities is like being tied to a mother's apron strings. When we were sent here, we were untied for the first time and set on our own. We were just daring to ask questions that we wouldn't have dared to ask around the older group. It was fun and exciting, and, at the same time, very scary. We asked some serious questions about our order, our communities, our backgrounds, our education, our identities.

Because we were a monastic order, we weren't involved with the laity. The structure was a sort of permanent retreat. All this was okay for me when I entered the order, but, as I got older, I began to ask myself if this life had really made me a better person. In the end, I felt that it had not.

Eventually, all but two of us in the Des Moines house left the religious life. Those who cared about us thought the reason we all left was because we ventured beyond the original structure. They saw it as a failure. But those of us who are on this side don't see it in terms of failure or success. We feel that we are on a journey, seeking, questioning, looking.

I don't mean to downgrade the religious lifestyle because it was good for me when I was at a young level of spirituality. I now have a different perspective about my relationship with God. I don't believe you can accumulate brownie points to cash in for some sort of trophy at the end of your life.

It took me forty-four years to realize that all the answers aren't going to be settled. Part of me was always looking for black and white answers, and I discovered that life is just not that way. Now I view life as a process of growth.

I entered religious life at nineteen and left in my early forties. It was all of my youth...all of my youth. I don't regret it. When I left, I had become convinced that I could be happy wherever I was, and I no longer felt it was necessary to be confined to one particular lifestyle. I felt that happiness had to be within you.

When the house was officially closed by the order, I, too, made the decisions to close the doors—temporarily. I was burned out. It was painful to watch this ten-year effort in Des Moines not work out the way we had dreamed.

I needed a break, so I went home to Santa Fe for a while. I had only planned to take a leave of absence. I had full intentions of going back. As time went on, I continued the questioning, the searching. I started feeling that life was more real outside the religious frame.

When I decided to make the leave permanent, my mother could not accept my decision. Because my situation was so hard on her, I decided to move back to Des Moines.

There was some security in deciding to come back to Des Moines because I had made some very good friends here. Some people, who I thought would be good friends, turned their backs on me. Others I didn't know well were very helpful and supportive.

I was naive. It did not register in my mind right away that I would have to work. I had a dowry to live on for awhile, but it soon began to dwindle. I had some idea of how much it cost to live because I took care of the expenses in the order for several women. The first time I bought groceries for myself, though, you would have thought I was feeding a monastery. I didn't know how to shop for one person.

I finally realized I was going to have to get a job. The only jobs I could imagine getting were cleaning bathrooms or selling hamburgers because I had been out of school for over twenty years. I began to panic. The monastery would call and ask if I needed anything, but I was too embarrassed to admit that I needed any help.

A friend encouraged me to apply for a state job. I remember the day I went into the state office building, standing in line with all these people and suddenly feeling like I was in the twilight zone. I wondered, "Who am I? What am I doing here?" A few months before, I was wearing a long religious robe, and I knew who I was then.

There was a glass wall in the building, and I saw the reflection of a woman in it. I watched this reflection a long time before I realized it was me. I didn't know it was me! I was completely shaken, just staring at this reflection. I thought, "My God, I'm really here in this state, in this building, with these clothes on"—I wasn't even sure how to dress—looking for a job. I was so overcome, I had to leave the building. I went flying down the street. It was so frightening!

That night at home all I could do was cry. I started to write a book about these experiences in the early weeks, but I had to stop. I didn't think anyone could understand.

In spite of it all, something in me said, "You just have to hang in there." As insecure as I was, I still had just enough confidence to keep going.

One day while I was job hunting downtown, I passed by a shoe store advertising a grand opening sale. I went in to browse and was amazed by so many colored shoes. It suddenly occurred to me that I could buy any color shoe I wanted, that I could buy a pair of shoes that were not black or white. When I realized this, I bought seven pairs of shoes: yellow, green, blue! It was the most wonderfully freeing experience.

I started dating...getting involved...took a psychology class...met people. And I began to get a feel for the thirst people have whether they are Christians or not—an innate need to pray, to meditate—to have some serious thoughts. In a monastic setting, our whole thrust is contemplation. But I have discovered that we are all contemplative. We all by nature want to take pauses, time for just being. It is something I have always understood, but not in depth.

I now work in an office setting that is very quiet, and I view this as God's protection of me. I also see patterns of behavior at work that repeat what I experienced in religious life, which has led me to conclude that we are all the same. No one group is more special than another. No one is on a pedestal. I feel wiser in this understanding.

At first, when I began to date, I was more like a nineteen-year-old than a forty-year-old. It was as though I had been frozen at age nineteen going into religious life and came out at the same age. When I thawed out, I found myself attracted to younger men, and then I realized that that just didn't add up. This was a mind-boggling discovery! When I met my husband, I thought he was an old man, and we are the same age.

Things happened to me at the convent that I didn't understand. Now that I look back, I understand it was my sexuality developing —and in all these other women as well. Now all that gets dealt with in some communities. In others, it's still taboo. It got complicated. I thought I was abnormal or something.

It has been hard on me to come to grips with my age. Because time stopped for me. You are kept very much a child in the convent. If you need soap, you ask for permission. And our ties are very strong. I still think I'm a "we."

When I first left, I kept wondering if I had done the right thing. I thought as long as I wondered, I must have made the wrong decision. I have come to accept that it is okay to wonder. I think many women make choices they will always question; they'll always wonder how their lives would have been if they had made other choices.

I have much gratitude for the experiences I have had in my forty-four years. I include the experiences that may not have been so wonderful. They were all necessary. Even my childhood when I was always witnessing struggle between my parents in their own journey. I feel more of an understanding that this is just the way life is.

I had been dating for quite a while when I met my husband John at a party. I thought he was too old for me. But after awhile, I began to come to terms with what age I really was. John is very good to me. I was fearful of getting married, but John has many qualities that have helped me gain respect for men. He is a mature man who is able to get involved with others, not just focus on himself. Most of the men I dated were very self-involved.

We are seriously considering having a child now. This is his second marriage, and he has children but is willing to have another if I really want this. Not having a child is the one regret I have about my life. I want to pick up where I left off, and I was childbearing age when I went into the convent. Part of me wants a child so much, but, realistically, I don't think I can handle it. My husband has a heart condition. If something happens to him, I wonder if I would be able to raise a child on my own.

And we want to travel. I want to go to Spain, to Barcelona where my great-grandfather was born. I may go back to school to become a certified counselor. I think I would like to work with others who may be considering a change like mine.

You know, many people say, "All my life I had a dream." I have had the satisfaction of following my dream. And now I sense there is even more to come.

Moxie and Rebecca
of Sunnybrook Farm

Saura Morris

> I used to feel like one of those inflatable punching bags.
> You knocked it down, and then it bounced back up ready
> to be hit again. I don't let myself get in situations like
> that anymore. I think about things now, I think about
> what's in it for me. When you are a salesperson, you
> have to convince customers that this service or product
> you're offering is of benefit. That's what you have to do
> for yourself, too.

Mutual friends told us we would enjoy meeting Saura Morris. "She's the Jewish Rebecca of Sunnybrook Farm," they said. "She's always up. She's the most positive person we know. She never has anything bad to say." What we discovered in our interview, though, was a woman for whom the term "moxie" could have been invented. Saura is a positive woman, true enough, but she has deliberately chosen her optimism in spite of the many difficulties and disappointments she has survived since childhood. And in spite of her fears about being alone and supporting herself in an uncertain economy.

Saura's story confirms that, while midlife women identify, pursue, and accomplish new goals, their achievements are not a guarantee of happiness. Sometimes old regrets and missed opportunities still linger. Sometimes new threats cloud recent successes.

But many midlife women seem to have an elastic sense of well being that allows them to handle threats much more comfortably than they did in earlier years. Instead of allowing themselves to become overwhelmed by fear, they become even more adept at risk-taking.

A desperate situation forced Saura, in her early forties, to take a risk for herself. She sold her home and left her family and friends in New York to move to St. Paul, Minnesota, where she has set about creating a rich new life.

Dressed in a black sweatsuit on which she has painted swirling designs in bright metallic paints, Saura lounges on an Oriental carpet in front of a brick fireplace as she tells us her story. She has a clear, musical voice and an enthusiastic laugh. As she talks, she occasionally pauses and wraps a long dark curl around her finger.

Saura Morris

I grew up in a small town in Vermont. My grandparents were Russian Jews who emigrated at the turn of the century. They settled in Vermont, probably because it was cold. It reminded them of Siberia where the Jews were chased by everybody during the pogroms. [She laughs.]

My father, Big Sam, was a gambler—a very handsome, charming, brilliant man who chose to do anything that was deceitful or devious. And that's how he really ran his life. He married my mother, if the story is true, because my grandparents offered him $10,000 to do it. My mother was a very shy twenty-year-old who had never dated and was scared of men.

They did marry, and it was the most improbable marriage. Because as shy and introverted as my mother was, here was my father, this very gregarious gambler who would take off for Cuba or Monte Carlo—all over the world—for months at a time.

My mother stayed with him, I think, because she didn't know where else to go. It was such a crazy life for us. We had very little money most of the time, and we would just wait for Big Sam to come back. I grew up thinking it was natural to open my father's underwear drawer and find a shoulder holster and gun and money—a lot of money, thousands of dollars.

I was nine when my father went to jail. Prior to that, we had lived in houses and normal neighborhoods, but this time he really went away, and, at the time, I thought that was probably the worst experience of my life. I spent the next three years with my mother visiting him. He was allowed to come out if he could get a job, but they didn't want him in Vermont, so we left for New York. And New York was where I spent the next thirty plus years.

It was very, very difficult to go from Vermont to New York. It was like going to another country. They didn't understand what I was saying, and I didn't understand what they were saying. I was twelve.

I was Jewish, but I grew up in such a crazy way that I said the rosary until I was nine. I sang in a Protestant church for two years. I celebrated everything. I always had a Christmas tree. I knew a little bit about a lot of religions. So here I was in New York, living in a town that was 90 percent Jewish. It was really tough.

The first time I remember being depressed was when we moved to New York. I was probably one of the few students who actually went down to the school counselor's office and asked if I could see her. I felt completely like a fish out of water. I didn't belong. I was very, very different from everybody. At least I thought so. I spoke differently, I looked different. I was fat. I had kinky hair and glasses. I had this funny accent that everybody made fun of. All of my life, I've always had an interest in people who come from foreign countries, probably because I felt I had come from a foreign country.

Even though we didn't have any money, we moved into this Long Island resort town that's on the ocean. Most of the people were very wealthy. The kids always had these cashmere sweater sets and poodle skirts and all these great '50s-era things.

My father had changed by then. He was embittered and ill. And abusive and violent. I had remembered him as this delightful figure who would come back periodically and bring me money and candy. Even the years he was in prison, I idealized him somewhat because I felt he had been put in there wrongly. I think you idealize parents who have left you or abandoned you.

But the brutal truth was, by the time we lived in New York, he was given to violent tempers, and he would hit me. He was not a well man. I was very depressed, and I was thirteen years old. I thought I'd never fit in, never belong. And then I spent the next thirty years making sure I would fit in.

At age thirteen, I became aware that the only way I could afford to be different from other children would have to be in ways that made me exceptional. I decided I better get rid of my accent. I was very artistic, I excelled in my classes. If I was eccentric, I was eccentric in the sense that people were sort of in awe of me. But I never, never felt like I belonged.

My father eventually lost his job, and I remember these horrible, chaotic conditions. He died when I was eighteen. I had just started college.

Three months later, I met David, who was to become my husband. I was not in love with David. I liked him. He was the first boy I met who was kind and trustworthy. So even though I was not in love with him, I decided he would make a good choice as a husband and father. Of course, I didn't have any idea what a good choice was, but David looked pretty good to me. He was middle class, he was a student, and he was going to become a teacher. His parents were middle class, they had tablecloths and dishes. It looked good.

I married David and—you talk about depression. I was married almost fourteen years, and I must have spent most of that time depressed. I couldn't get up in the morning. I hated being a housewife. I didn't understand what I had done. I was angry with myself, I was angry with him. The marriage was a mess. We had two children, and that was the only thing we agreed on. We both adored our children.

It was a bad marriage for a lot of reasons. I was one of them. Maybe because I was unrealistic about what my expectations were. I really wanted to feel that romantic love you read about, and I didn't. He wanted a wife who liked to make meals and do all the proper things. And I didn't want to do that either, so both of us were looking for the wrong thing.

He had an affair when we had been married about nine years. The marriage lasted another four or five years, and then we divorced.

All my life I had feared being alone, and there I was, alone, with two children. My mother was sickly, so I had to spend a lot of time taking care of her. She lived about fifty miles from me, I would go back and forth seeing her all the time.

I became involved in a relationship with a married man. The good thing about the relationship was that I really loved him, and I loved him for many years. The bad thing was that I stayed far too long in a dead-end relationship. One of the reasons I stayed so long was that Don thought I was beautiful, wonderful, all the right things.

I was afraid to go out and see what the world was like. One of the first times I went out after I was divorced, I was terrified. When I got out of the relationship with Don, though, ten years later, I vowed I would never go out with a married man again.

Then I got involved with this terrible man. It was the craziest thing when I think about it now. I answered a personal ad, and it turned out to be Bernie, this crazy, but fascinating man. He was Israeli, he was an artist, he was a crazy, volatile con man. He reminded me of my father. I think I got involved with him because I thought I could save him. I was not able to save my father, but now I had a second chance.

Bernie was so horrible, and he cost me so much money that I had to sell my house. He ran up my charge plates well over $10,000, and he threatened to kill my children. Subsequently, I've read about other women who have been victimized like this.

Bernie thought I would sell the house and take off with him, but what happened was [she smiles] I sold the house and took off with myself.

I could have stayed where I was, I could have sold my house and got an apartment and continued meeting these horrible men like Bernie or other married men or whatever, but, for the first time in my life, I said to myself, "This is an opportunity. I don't have to stay here. I can go on and take a risk. My problem is that I haven't taken any risk up to now."

I was forty-three or forty-four. I realized that it was probably my last chance to do something. If I stayed in New York, if I stayed where I was, I felt I would die. I had no goals, no hopes of anything better.

I was making destructive choices in friends—not only men, but women, too. I would tend to get involved with people who needed help. We would commiserate together, negative behaviors.

I spent a lot of time investigating St. Paul and Minnesota. I have family here, and that was one of the things that propelled me to move here. I had visited a few times, and it reminded me of the place I grew up in. I wanted to go to a small city that would offer me opportunity for culture and yet have the accessibility that I didn't have on Long Island.

The worst thing was that I left my children in New York. My older daughter had started college, and my younger daughter had already moved to her father's a few years earlier. I felt guilty leaving them, but I knew I had to move. I knew it was the right thing.

I wasn't used to doing things for me, so moving here was the most important, the first big thing I did for me. I knew I wouldn't be any good to anybody if I didn't survive. I knew I had to change my life.

The worst fear I had was about what I was going to do for work. I got a sales job about six weeks after I got here. Working in the Midwest was strange. All the years I lived in New York, I thought of myself as a Vermonter. And now people in Minnesota treated me like I was a New Yorker. I'm generalizing, but the people you do business with here are much less direct. Their demeanor is so different. One has to be more subtle, much more courteous. I had to learn how to be aggressive in New York because I really wasn't, and, when I came here, I had to learn not to be aggressive. All these confusing things and issues.

The way I dressed, the way I talked, and my age were bigger issues than I had been used to. When I first moved here, I applied for an insurance job that probably no one in the world was better qualified for than I was because I had worked in insurance many years after my divorce.

I went into this insurance office, and they were looking for the same kind of experience that I had. Two or three times during the interview, they asked me if I would mind working with young people. I was very pleasant about it. I looked around the office, and it was big—maybe sixty or seventy people—and I realized that everyone in that office was young. I called up the next week and was told that they had given the position to someone else.

I said, "I want to know who you gave the job to, and I want to know their age," and they started to get so nervous. They said, "Oh, it wasn't that." So I asked what qualifications the person they hired had that I didn't have. They hemmed around. I had never let age be an issue when I looked for a job, but here I was.

Finally, I sort of fell into this account executive position with this company that was just dying to hire a middle-aged Jewish New Yorker, and there

I was. But I still worry about that, about my age. It's hard enough to go out to look for a job these days. And my company has lost a lot of business in the last couple of years.

When I moved here, I had a little money left, and I wanted to buy a house or a condominium if I could. I bought this condo in two weeks' time. I narrowed it all down. I am very organized. I saw this place, and I walked into it and asked the woman how much it was, and she told me. I said, "All right I'll take it." She looked at me strangely, the real estate agent. But it was the right size, and my cat could play in the back courtyard. I hate cooking—and that's the smallest kitchen you could have next to a hot plate.

I had never lived alone before. I had always lived with either my parents, my husband, my children, or roomers in my house to help pay the bills. At first, living alone was terrible. I used to cry every night. I missed my children. I missed my friends. I decided I had to make a concerted effort to be comfortable, or else I would go crazy. Then I began to learn to like living alone.

I really love this place. It feels right. I decorated it the way I wanted to. Now I think, "Gee, you're really living by yourself, and it's not so bad, is it?"

People say my condo is like a museum because I have so much art in here—paintings, all these artifacts from all over the world. These are interesting things to me, things I love, things that are fun.

I didn't decorate when I was a housewife. When I was first married, I had so little feeling of what I was and who I was. And I never grew up in a house that was decorated. I used to follow tradition. If everybody had Spanish, I had Spanish. Whatever they had, I had. But it wasn't mine. This is me. I don't care if other people like my pieces. If I had to live in one room, I would want to live in one room filled with art, interesting things from our own country and different countries.

I've created a whole new life for myself since I moved here. I do a lot of things here—go to the theater, concerts, flea markets, festivals. In New York, I didn't do anything, I was miserable, depressed all the time. I spent ten years of my life just waiting for this married man to come visit me.

Here, I've made a conscious decision to get involved with positive people. When I first came here, I met this woman who wanted someone to go to bars with. When I was in New York, I had these friends who were neurotic, and we would share our misery. And I said, "I'm not going to do that anymore," and I have not done that here.

I've done more in the last few years than I had done for many, many years. I take art classes at a community center. I really wanted to be an artist when I was younger. I don't feel I have enough talent to do it professionally, but I do work in art. For example, I've painted wall murals for people, for children's bedrooms. Sometimes, I sell enamel pieces I make at craft fairs. I've met some really great people through my creativity.

Through my friend Barbara, I met some interesting people in the black community. One of them commissioned me to do a couple paintings of Jesus and Ezekiel. The paintings came out great, and I was asked to present them at the church. The parishioners were so excited about this Jewish woman who had done these paintings. It was a Baptist church that laid hands on people. They had drums and the most wonderful music. That's how I became the leading middle-aged Jewish painter of Christian themes in this community.

About six months ago, I decided to get involved with the Big Sister program. My years with my own children were cut off by circumstances and geography, but I still needed that closeness. It's like ghosts of experience that aren't ready to make their peace. Also, I felt like I had been a child of a single parent, and that's what being a Big Sister is about. My Little Sister's father died when she was seven. She has several siblings, and sometimes I take all of them. It's like having a family, they're adorable kids.

I met my current boyfriend through a woman I became acquainted with when I first moved here. He and I don't have an ideal relationship, but we do have a comfortable one. He's a great companion, a very good man, and he loves to do a lot of things. That's fine because I like to do everything.

The most exciting thing about being almost fifty is that I don't feel it in a lot of ways. This sort of leads up to why I had plastic surgery very recently. I had the bags under my eyes removed. They run in my family, those bags.

In spite of all my insecurities, I always knew I had this beautiful face. I had worked as a photographer's model when I was young. And then all of a sudden, I didn't have that face either. It was really scary.

It's not like losing or gaining weight. You can always go on a diet. But what do you do with your face? You can't go to Nutri Systems for your face. I didn't expect to wake up after surgery looking twenty-five. I expected to look better than I did. And I do, I like the changes. Some parts of my face are still numb, but it's getting better.

How you look is very, very important in business—especially when you're an account executive. I don't think I'll ever look like a model, but I was looking very old, I thought, and tired. I've been sick for the last few years. After years of problems that no one could seem to diagnose properly, I had a hysterectomy last winter. I think the physical problems made me look older, too.

The reality is that employers don't value older employees. I'm an account executive, and I have to think about that—maybe not in my current job, but what about tomorrow? The economy isn't great these days. It's just easier for companies to hire young people. One of my clients seems to hire only young, thin blondes.

And it's true that men in business just pay more attention, have more interest in younger women. I mean professionally, not sexually. For example, they will take the time to go out to lunch with young female vendors.

I'm not sure where I'm going from here, but I think it will be easier going there. My fears right now are very realistic. I am concerned about supporting myself. But whatever my fear, I know I can survive. I have survived a lot of things. You get better at surviving your fears over the years.

I used to feel like one of those inflatable punching bags. You knocked it down, and then it bounced back up ready to be hit again. I don't let myself get in situations like that anymore. I think about things now, I think about what's in it for me. When you are a salesperson, you have to convince customers that this service or product you're offering is of benefit. That's what you have to do for yourself, too.

Firecracker

Joyce Clements

> I used to think that, because something was interesting, that was enough reason to be involved with it....But I've learned over my life that not everything interesting is worthwhile. The way to lead a satisfying life is to find those things that are fulfilling to you, that you can give your best to....You need to find something that allows you to be a good person...the fulfillment of a life is to be as creative and open as possible.

For jeweler and sculptor Joyce Clements (her real name), play is serious business. That's only natural since she was born on the Fourth of July and, as a child, thought that the Fourth was a holiday in her honor. She continues to celebrate her birthday in appropriate style: For her fiftieth birthday this past July, she threw an aerial party where friends were invited to try their luck and agility on the trapeze. Joyce, a veteran of several months' practice, briefly performed with her instructor.

A trapeze bar hangs in the middle of Joyce's studio, which overlooks the ocean off the coast of Bolinas, California. On one side is her jeweler's bench where she creates one-of-a-kind pieces in metals and precious and semi-precious gems. The other half of the studio is dedicated to metal sculpture, which Joyce began about a year ago partly because she wanted to explore her creativity in a new art form.

Joyce is an energetic woman with a lifelong appetite for learning and challenging herself. She earned a bachelor's degree in philosophy, a master's degree in sociology, and a doctorate in criminology. She originally started making jewelry as a way of dealing with the stresses of graduate school; she became a professional jeweler in her late thirties because of a need to do something "creative and positive" with her life.

Although she gave up the social sciences as a profession, Joyce is still very committed to contributing to the social good. And she has discovered original ways to fulfill her commitment since she moved to Bolinas around the age of forty. For example, she has served as president of the board of directors of the Bolinas Museum since 1989 and, for three years prior, was the start-up director of the museum.

Joyce speculates that she will spend the next ten years growing as an artist and community activist. She wants to create sculptures that will communicate important messages about society to the public. She dreams about organizing a network of midlife professionals willing to donate some of their time and talent to social organizations. But she also wants to remember to play because "playing is very important for everyone." After spending only a morning with Joyce, we found ourselves leaving with the hope that we would be included on the guest list for her sixtieth birthday party.

Joyce Clements

I was born in 1942 in Washington, D.C., on the Fourth of July. The date is significant because, growing up, I always thought the Fourth was a celebration for me. My parents owned a little variety store in Virginia, and they always had a fireworks stand. When I was old enough—probably seven or eight—I helped sell the fireworks. And I loved it.

Of course, there were always lots of fireworks left over. We had the biggest Fourth of July celebration of any private family around.

My parents were very energetic people. They didn't come from a very well-educated background, but they made up for it in self-motivation. I've always admired them a lot. They were very scrappy and worked very hard to get what they wanted, and it resulted in a fulfilling life for them.

Because my parents worked so hard, I was raised without much supervision. I think that's an important factor in my life because I had the opportunity to make decisions at a very early age. I spent a lot of time alone. I've always been active and interested in games and sports and creative things.

When I was in the seventh or eighth grade, I started a community newspaper. We lived close to the county courthouse, and there was a building there where all of the reporters who had that beat had desks. They would collect the news and sit down and type it up on the spot. I hung out there and watched them and asked endless questions. I learned how to type. My parents had a booklet that went with their typewriter, so I just practiced until I could type well enough to prepare the mimeographs for my own paper.

I think I sold my newspapers for five cents apiece. I took ads, did all the drawings, typed and mimeographed and stapled the paper, and then sold it. It was fun, and I felt very important. People in the neighborhood would talk to me about it seriously. When I was stuck with an empty column, someone would give me a recipe I could use. I kept the paper going for about two years or so.

My father did a lot of mechanical things. He worked on cars and could fix anything. I wanted him to teach me how to do this stuff, but he refused. He said that was not what girls did. I was furious about that. I always watched him anyway. He couldn't stop me from watching him. [She laughs.]

In high school, I played sports virtually every day of the week—softball and basketball. I wasn't sure that I wanted to go to college. I didn't know one college from another.

You know those bookcovers you can buy and put on your books? I bought one that said Duke University. I liked the sound, I liked the bookcover. I looked up a little bit about Duke, and it sounded cool. I talked to the counselor about it, and she said, "You could never get into Duke University." At first, I was hurt, and then I was mad. I don't know why she said that. I had really great grades and lots of extracurricular activities.

I made up my mind at that point that, if I went to college, I was going to Duke University. And I got in. I consider that one of the great things that happened to me because Duke is a fabulous school. Very intellectually stimulating. I'd always loved to read, I was a library kind of kid. At Duke, I met people who were fascinating, really bright. I felt intellectually energized and challenged.

I started in zoology because I wanted to be a doctor at that point. But actually my favorite courses were history and philosophy. I eventually switched to philosophy. I can still see myself in this phone booth explaining to my father that I was changing my major from zoology to philosophy. I don't remember what his words were exactly, something to the effect of "What the hell is that?" He asked what I was going to do with it. I probably didn't give him a very good explanation. I just wanted to do it. In philosophy, you could explore and reconceptualize things a million different ways and have these interesting conversations with people.

When I graduated, the problem of what to do with a philosophy degree became paramount. I went back to Arlington, Virginia, and started applying for jobs—anything I could find. Since I always liked to read, I thought the Library of Congress sounded great. I got what had to be the world's worst job—filing index cards at the Library for the millions of books that get published in the world every day.

They had this room set up that was probably the size of two football fields. Tables lined up and down in rows. And they gave kids like me little stools with wheels, and we used to scoot up and down rows and file these cards alphabetically. It paid $5200 a year in 1964.

I asked my supervisor, "What's the next job here?" She told me that, when someone could do 120 cards an hour, she would get a raise. I grabbed those cards and ran up and down those rows like crazy, right? Then I told her

I did it, and she said, "You've got to be able to do it for six months." I quit the next day.

My next job was in community recreation planning. I worked hard, and I loved helping develop opportunities for other people to play and learn and have fun. My boss thought I should have some official education in recreation, so she sponsored my going to graduate school. As it turned out, I got hooked on the sociology courses that were a part of it, especially the courses on deviance and criminology.

The head of the sociology department said I should think about getting a Ph.D. I had always wanted to come to the West Coast, and there was a school of criminology at the University of California, Berkeley. I thought I would get a Ph.D. and teach at the university level. I was idealistic—I thought being a professor would keep me intellectually active.

I really got a big dose of the good-old-boy scene at Berkeley. And I also got a good dose of how professors got grants to do research projects and then used graduate students at slave wages to do the research and writing—without giving them any credit for it. It seemed like first-class extortion to me, and I didn't want to have any part of it.

While I was in graduate school, I was also the editor-in-chief of an international publication on criminology. Being the editor taught me a lot of business skills. I also learned a lot about academia that disillusioned me. A visiting professor submitted an article for the journal that turned out to be plagiarized. I was really upset about it. I took the problem to the faculty, and they just decided to ignore it.

I am a very honest person, and I think the only way for all of us to have any quality in our lives is to treat each other honestly and with honor. When I saw what I considered one of the biggest academic crimes you could commit totally accepted without repercussions, I realized that I didn't want to continue to be involved in academia.

A friend of mine in graduate school was going out with a guy who was a jeweler. I really missed doing things with my hands, and he was broke and wanted to give some lessons. I went over to his workshop two or three times a week to watch him and ask questions. I figured out what tools I would need and bought them to get started. I set up a little studio in my apartment and started making things and realized how much I loved it.

I studied like crazy for my orals, and I passed them, but then I went into a deep depression. I had put so much energy into the work, I felt like I had fallen off a cliff. I'm not normally a depressive person. Doing jewelry and being outdoors were really healing experiences. I started doing more and more jewelry.

Finally, I started working on my dissertation. The name of it was "Beyond the Rhetoric: the Dynamics of Repression in the 1934 Maritime and General Strike in San Francisco." The '70s were a very politically active time. I was one of those people in Sproul Plaza when the helicopters came swooping down and spraying tear gas because of our protests about Vietnam. A very radicalizing experience. This made me interested in repression, how people could be prevented from expressing their feelings, their rage.

The dissertation was completely involving and fun—most of the time anyway. Probably the most I learned in graduate school was from doing my own research and writing. I came to know the guts of history, what it means to reconstruct, to decide the facts. I got a small grant from some federal agency to travel around the country to libraries to do research. I did oral histories and read letters and documents until I forgot that I was living in the '70s. As soon as I finished the dissertation, I got calls from several universities asking if I wanted to teach, but I said no.

After some private consulting work, I took a job as head of a jail-improvement research project. I accepted the position because I was still looking for something worthwhile to do, and this research sounded like it had some positive value. My office was a jail cell right in the jail block. It was pretty unnerving being behind bars and within seeing, hearing, and smelling distance of a high-security scene. I came to this job as a political radical. I thought that every prisoner was basically a political prisoner.

From doing the research, though, I learned that not every prisoner is a political prisoner. I learned that there are some really rotten people. I did a lot of interviewing with my utopian ideas. Prisoners would tell me what good persons they were—and then I would go to my computer and pull out rap sheets on them that were ten yards long. I also had a lot of dealings with the sheriff's department, and they were hard, disillusioned people, many of them alcoholic. And I felt I was becoming an alcoholic. I was starting to drink a lot.

One day, my partner, whom I've been with for twenty-eight years, said, "Why don't you quit?" And I said, "I've got all these years into this education, all this money into this education, and I'm getting paid a fantastic salary." And she said, "So what? You're unhappy." So I quit.

I had great potential in the criminology field. I had good offers to teach, to work. It was hard to say no. But I made the decision to quit, and I knew I was doing the right thing. I started making jewelry, something I had no training for. By most accounts, it was an insane move. But I have never looked back, never. I was in my late thirties at this time.

One day around Thanksgiving of that year, two friends and I saw a Chinese market that was going out of business in Berkeley. We spontaneously decided to lease the space to open a retail jewelry business. We decided to open up before Christmas, right? The place was painted institutional green, had fluorescent lights all over, it was horrible. We worked twenty-four hours a day to get that place open, built our own showcases—the whole bit—and we did get it open in two weeks.

Between us, we had thirteen thousand dollars. Within a couple of years, though, the store was grossing over a hundred thousand dollars a year. In 1978, that was great, but I was working way too hard. I was the only person making jewelry, and I was the manager and marketing chief, all rolled into one. I decided I was having to rush too much to be able to make the jewelry pieces I wanted to do. I was beginning to repeat myself. I was beginning to doubt my creativity. I decided to sell my interest in the store.

My partner and I took the small chunk of money we made from the store and bought this place in Bolinas in 1981. We had been coming out here every weekend for years just to walk on the beach. Every Sunday evening when it was time to go, I would look around and say, "Those people are so lucky who get to live here. I wish we could just go up there and walk into one of those houses."

This is the most peaceful place I've ever lived. For the first year or two, I vowed I would always be here to see the sun go down. And I was. There was a time when I felt so peaceful here that I felt like my pulse—this might sound ridiculous—but like my pulse and the pulse of the earth were the same.

Seeing the sun go down here makes me feel connected to the earth. There's something so magnificent about it. Frequently, when the sun sets, you're treated to successive changes of shape, something to do with the atmosphere. A few years ago, I did a series of rings called "Sun Temples" based on this phenomenon. Before I moved here, I didn't even realize that the sun changes its position throughout the year. Twice a year, it sets directly in front of my window. In California, there aren't any seasons really, so, to me, the seasons are the sun and the different types of light it brings out in summer and in winter.

I'll never be rich making jewelry. I have supported myself although the recession has made it hard the last several years. If I didn't have a partner who is making good money, I probably couldn't have stuck with it through the lows.

Here's where the real payoff is. I am getting paid a high salary in terms of my own freedom. I get to dress like I want, I can do and be the person I want to be. Best of all, I have the privilege of making real whatever I conceptualize. I'm a hard taskmaster. I work a full day every single day, but, nevertheless, I'm the one who makes the decisions about my business and my life.

I realize I can't control as much as I thought I could when I was young. I used to think I could. There comes a point in life when you have to recognize that you can control very little. You can control, to a certain degree, what you do to and with yourself. If you're not doing what's right for yourself, your body will tell you so.

If I'm not doing something that I'm happy doing or that's right for me, I know it everywhere. I know it in my body, I know it in my soul. I've always intuitively been aware of this, but I trust my intuition more now. I used to barge past my feelings if I made up my mind to do something. Now I'm getting better at saying no to my mind, at stopping to feel things out. I think that's one of the best parts about getting older.

I used to think that, because something was interesting, that was enough reason to be involved with it. I was fascinated by the ideas of social science, and I just went with them. But I've learned over my life that not everything interesting is worthwhile. The way to lead a satisfying life is to find those things that are fulfilling to you, that you can give your best to, that you can see results in. You need to find something that allows you to be a good person, to make a contribution—but not just for other people. The fulfillment of a life is to be as creative and open as possible.

Now, I'm beginning metal sculpture. I'm taking a welding class, and I'm the only woman in a class of twenty-five men, but they are coming to accept me. In a way, it's crazy to be doing something that takes such upper body strength at this age.

But one reason I'm interested in sculpture is that I think I know how to do everything in jewelry I want to do, so I don't need to keep doing it. Another reason is that the products I make in jewelry are enjoyed only by one person and that person's friends. There's nothing wrong with that, but I would like to make some pieces that more people will be able to see and relate to. And I don't want to have to do only things that are beautiful, I don't want to be stuck with beauty. I want to expand my possibilities and my opportunity to make statements.

I'm not going to give up jewelry entirely. I'm still going to do commissions and pieces I want to do. For example, I recently finished a series of four gold neck pieces that are based on my conception of the Greek myth about the judgment of Paris who was forced to pick the most beautiful goddess on Mount Olympus. I've made four pieces, one for each of the three goddesses, and also the golden apple.

I'm doing a sculpture series called "Conviction" that's a statement on rigidity. I'm working on a piece now that's steel and plexiglass and other kinds of metals. It's basically an elevated square head of plexiglass that you can see inside of. On top of the head is a bed. The idea is that, if you hold onto the conviction, if by making your bed, you feel you have to lie in it, you are imprisoning yourself. I'm also working on a playful sculpture series that celebrates fun. The first piece is called the Juggler, and it incorporates several pieces that move in the wind.

About a year ago, I started taking trapeze lessons from a woman in town. For my fiftieth birthday, this past July, my partner and I rented a trapeze studio in Berkeley and decided to throw an aerial party. We invited about forty-five people. I've never performed on a stage or anything, and I was nervous, but I did a little performance at the party with my instructor. Fortunately, I didn't kill myself.

I can't tell you how happy it made me to see forty-five friends at ten o'clock on a Sunday morning in a gym doing stretching exercises and trying the trapeze. We also had some clowns who taught people ground-based things to do if they were afraid to try the trapeze. It was a great celebration.

I'm going to have a great birthday when I'm sixty, too. I have to see what emerges between fifty and sixty, but, I guarantee you, it will have something to do with play. I will abandon myself to joy. Play is important to me. I think it should be important to everybody.

Bibliography

Bateson, Mary Catherine. *Composing a Life*. New York: Penguin Books, 1989.

Bolen, Jean Shinoda. *Wise-Woman Archetype: Menopause as Initiation*. Sounds True Recordings, A137, 1991.

Christ, Carol P. *Diving Deep and Surfacing*. Boston: Beacon Press, 1986.

Gilligan, Carol. *In a Different Voice: Psychological Theory and Women's Development*. Cambridge: Harvard University Press, 1982.

Goleman, Daniel, *et al.The Creative Spirit*. New York: Penguin Books USA Inc., 1992.

Grudin, Robert. *The Grace of Great Things: Creativity and Innovation*. New York: Ticknor and Fields, 1990.

Hancock. Emily. *The Girl Within*. New York: Fawcett Columbine, 1989.

Heilbrun, Carolyn. *Writing a Woman's Life*. New York: W. W. Norton and Company, 1988.

Hjelle, Larry A., and Daniel J. Ziegler. "Erik Erikson: Psychosocial Theory of Personality." *Personality Theories*. New York: McGraw-Hill Book Company, 1981. 113-150.

Kumin, Maxine. "Archeology of a Marriage." In Heilbrun, Carolyn G. *Writing a Woman's Life*. New York: W. W. Norton and Company, 1988. (For the complete text of the poem, see Kumin, Maxine. *The Retrieval System*. New York: Penguin Books, 1978.)

May, Rollo. *The Courage to Create*. Toronto: George McLeod Limited, 1975.

Malta, Ann. Personal interview. 27 April 1992.

Miller, Jean Baker. *Toward a New Psychology of Women*. Boston: Beacon Press, 1986.

Rountree, Cathleen. *Coming into Our Fullness: On Women Turning Forty*. Freedom, CA: The Crossing Press, 1991.

Sinetar, Marsha. *Living Happily Ever After*. New York: Dell Publishing, 1990.

Steinem, Gloria. *Revolution From Within: A Book of Self-Esteem*. Boston: Little, Brown and Company, 1992.

U.S. Bureau of the Census. *Current Population Report*. Series P-25, Nos. 1045-1057.